HOW HAIG SAVED LENIN

How Haig Saved Lenin

Brian Pearce

Foreword by
Evan Mawdsley

M
MACMILLAN
PRESS

First published 1987

Published by
THE MACMILLAN PRESS LTD
Houndmills, Basingstoke, Hampshire RG21 2XS
and London
Companies and representatives
throughout the world

Typeset by Wessex Typesetters
(Division of The Eastern Press Ltd)
Frome, Somerset

Printed in Hong Kong

British Library Cataloguing in Publication Data
Pearce, Brian, *1915–*
How Haig saved Lenin.
1. World War, 1914–1918
I. Title
940.3 D521
ISBN 0–333–43261–4

The recollection of German strength in the World War is still alive everywhere.

(The German Ambassador in Moscow reporting on 6 September 1939 to the German Foreign Office on the state of public opinion in the Soviet capital as Hitler's troops advanced into Poland, *Documents on German Foreign Policy*, series D, vol. VIII, [1954] Document 13)

Contents

List of Maps

Foreword

Evan Mawdsley

The First World War and the Russian Revolution were giant events, and giant events lead to giant myths. Some myths appeared almost immediately, while others unfolded over time. They came partly from revulsion at the cost of the 'Great War', and partly from popular hopes for a better world; myths, of course, have an element of truth. They came also from the propaganda of German ultra-nationalists and, at the other extreme, of Soviet and non-Soviet Communist parties. About the World War there were the myths of the utter futility of trench warfare, of the incompetence of the generals on both sides, and of the 'stab in the back' which destroyed the German Army. About the Revolution there were the myths of the International, of the pure new order created by the Bolsheviks, of the political and diplomatic skill of Lenin, and of the imperialist intervention by the Allies. All these myths are challenged, at least to some extent, in this book, but more effectively demolished is the myth that the way in which war ended on the Russian Front helped to destroy Germany and allowed the Allied victory.

Part of the fascination of the year 1918, one reason it bred so many myths, was that it was so much of a turning point, real or potential. Unlike 1944–5 it seemed possible even in the summer of 1918 that the battles could go either way, that German hegemony was still possible. And at the same time the spectre of European Revolution had more substance at the end of the First World War than it would ever have again. Very few leaders, in Moscow, in Berlin, in London, in Paris, could know how history was going to unfold. The element of 'might have been' was very strong, and to understand the way people behaved in 1918 it is more than usually necessary for the historian to forget hindsight and think back to a time when the whole world seemed to hang in the balance. This is one of the strengths of the present book.

For all its pivotal nature, however, 1918 has not attracted much attention from recent generations of historians. The war itself, perhaps because Allied victory achieved so little at such great cost and because it left so many problems for the future, is not a fashionable area of study. And for many historians of the Russian

Revolution the era comes to an end with the October Revolution, or perhaps with the peace of Brest-Litovsk in March 1918. It is remarkable that the standard history of the Civil War was written over fifty years ago by W. H. Chamberlin; only now is more being written about the subject. Even so, the chaotic year of 1918, when the Bolsheviks had only a weak grasp on power, is still relatively little studied; historians in both East and West seem happier with the heroic revolutionary upheaval of 1917 or the achievements of the consolidated Soviet State in 1919–20. The present volume makes an important contribution to filling that gap.

Finally, historians of the Russian Revolution and historians of the World War have lived in self-contained worlds. Brian Pearce in this present book performs the great service of bringing these two worlds together. He does so with a rare combination of abilities. His knowledge of the period and the subject is deep; he is best known for his many scholarly translations, especially the five volumes of Trotsky's collected military writings. He has a fascination with the riddles of the revolutionary era, as well as the qualities needed to find the answers: remarkable scholarly patience and the energy to follow clues in many directions. But it is not enough to have mastered the sources; he has an ear for those historical disharmonies which demand investigation. When there is added to this a strong and subtle sense of irony – as expressed in the title, *How Haig Saved Lenin* – it is clear that Brian Pearce's book will be read with great interest.

Evan Mawdsley
University of Glasgow

Preface

In writing this book I have been greatly helped by three historians in particular – Winfried Baumgart, Richard K. Debo and John Terraine – both through their published work and through private correspondence. They bear no responsibility, of course, for the views expressed by me.

The idea of the book came to me when travelling by coach from Calais to Paris. The coach stopped, for the passengers to get refreshment and exercise, at a village called La Targette, where there is a British military cemetery of the First World War. Walking among the graves I noticed that the men buried there had mostly been killed in the first months of the great German offensive of 1918. I dedicate the essay to their memory.

B.P.

Acknowledgements

The quotations from Cabinet (CAB), Foreign Office (FO) and War Office (WO) records, which are Crown-copyright, appear by permission of the Controller of HM Stationery Office.

This work was made possible by a grant from the Lipman Trust and an award from the British Academy.

1 A Soviet Myth

November 1918 saw the surrender of Imperial Germany to the Allied Powers and also the first anniversary of the Bolshevik Government in Russia, which, to the surprise of many, friends as well as foes, had survived for several months longer than the Paris Commune. Was there any connection between these two historic events? To some Soviet historians the answer is clear: Germany's defeat was due mainly or largely to the impact of Bolshevism upon the German armed forces.

An outspoken expression of this view is to be found in I. I. Rostunov's *Russkii front pervoi mirovoi voiny* (1976) where we read (p. 385):

> Bourgeois writers, distorting historical facts, try to show that Germany's defeat in the First World War resulted from the operations of the British and French forces on the Western Front. They particularly emphasise the importance of the counter-offensive by the Allied forces in 1918. In actual fact, the fighting capacity of the German armies had been broken long before that operation, and no small role in their weakening had been played by the Russian front. An immense influence on the undermining of the fighting capacity of the German armed forces was exercised by the ideas of the Great October Revolution, which the German soldiers returning from Soviet Russia brought back with them.

The same idea is put forward, somewhat less aggressively, in *Istoriya pervoi mirovoi voiny 1914–1918 gg.* (1975), edited by the same Rostunov: 'The Great October Socialist Revolution had enormous influence on the course and outcome of the campaign [in France in 1918]' (vol. 2, p. 533). Nor is Rostunov its only proponent.[1] A. A. Akhtamzyan, in the first volume of *Istoriya mezhdunarodnykh otnoshenii i vneshnei politiki SSSR 1917–1967 gg.* (1967: general editor, V. G. Trukhanovskii) writes (p. 54) of the 'immense role' played in the failure of the German offensive of March 1918 by 'the influence of the October Revolution in lowering the fighting capacity' of the German forces. And in *Istoriya grazhdanskoy voiny v SSSR*, vol. 3 (1957: edited by S. F. Naida and others) we find 'the growth in influence of the policy of the Soviet Government' mentioned as a major reason why 'Germany began to suffer severe defeats on the Western Front' (p. 278). Even where the contribution to Germany's defeat made by the Allied armies receives mention, some writers see fit to give equal billing to the 'Bolshevism factor': for example, E. Putyrskii, in *Boevoi Petrograd v 1918 godu* (1972) tells his readers that the defeat of the German forces on the Western front was due 'not only to the superiority of the forces of the Anglo-American [*sic*] bloc but also to the influence on the German soldiers of the ideas of October . . . .' (pp. 112–13).

This way of presenting the relation between the Allied victory on the Western Front and the survival of the Soviet Government in Russia through 1918 has a long record, going back even to a time before the treaty of Brest-Litovsk. In a conversation with Prince Bibesco on 31 December 1917, Chicherin said:

> People are always talking to us about the destruction of Prussian militarism, which we more than anyone else wish for. But there is more than one way to destroy Prussian militarism. There is the brute force which the Allies have now been employing for over 41 months. There are also ideas which can be introduced into Germany.[2]

René Marchand reported a talk he had with A. A. Sol'ts at Smolny about the same time, when the Bolshevik said:

> Even from your imperialist point of view you ought to agree, if you were really impartial, that by our example, our close proximity and our ceaseless activity we have already done towards weakening Germany's military strength, and consequently bringing about the military victory of your arms – for which, of course, we are not working – much more than all the Ruzskys, Brusilovs and other butchers whose brilliant services have been hailed in your press. You complain that Germany has been enabled to concentrate all her forces on your front. But you forget that the troops Germany is transferring from our front have already been greatly affected by our propaganda. . . .[3]

Kamenev, interviewed by a Swedish journal on 13 February 1918, opined that 'the German troops freed by the peace with Russia will produce a favourable pressure on the Western Front for peace'.[4]

When, in August 1918, it became apparent to everyone that the tide had turned against Germany on the Western Front, Lenin hastened to explain what had happened by the influence of Bolshevism: 'What the German diplomats joked about – the "Russification" of the German soldiers – now turns out to be no joke at all, but the bitter truth. The spirit of protest is rising, "treason" is becoming a common thing in the German army.'[5] Experience was justifying, in his view, the claim he had made on 28 June that, by the armistice with Germany and the peace of Brest-Litovsk, 'the workers' and peasants' government has done more than any other government in the world to weaken the German imperialists . . .'.[6] A few days before the Western armistice, on 6 November, Lenin asserted that 'the German army proved to be useless and unfit for action . . . because the soldiers who refused to fight were transferred from the Eastern Front to the German Western Front and carried with them what the bourgeoisie call world Bolshevism'.[7] And, towards the end of 1918, he claimed that it was 'contact with Soviet Russia' that had 'started in this army of German working people the process of disintegration which was to make itself felt a few months later'.[8]

The idea thus formulated at once became the standard explanation of Germany's defeat in Left-wing circles in Britain and America. It possessed, of course, the twofold attractiveness of (a) countering the charge that the Bolsheviks had 'let down' Russia's allies and (b) depriving the British and American 'militarists' of credit for the outcome of the war. Ironically, by contradicting the official Allied explanation that the German army had simply been defeated by superior generalship on the Allied side, and emphasising the role played by Bolshevism, it strengthened the propaganda of the nationalist extreme-Right element in Germany, who held that their country's defeat had been due entirely to a 'stab in the back' administered by 'the Reds'.

Albert Rhys Williams, testifying before a US Senate Committee in February 1919, associated himself with the view that 'Bolshevik propaganda had as much to do with the sudden collapse of Germany as our military operations',[9] and Frank Keddie, of the Society of Friends, testifying a few days later, also dwelt upon the theme of Bolshevik propaganda among German troops on the Eastern Front: 'Then they ordered the German troops over to the other front, and the troops said they had had enough, and a revolution broke out in the interior of Germany, and the Bolsheviks saved 500 000 American lives.'[10] Morgan Philips Price wrote in 1919, referring to the German offensive of March 1918:

The Soviet Government of Russia is accused of being responsible for this onslaught: but I submit that its tactics formed an important part of the armoury which finally broke the power of Prussian militarism. The very fact that the politically non-conscious elements of the German people got a taste of peace on the East front broke their will to war. 'If we can have peace with Russia,' they instinctively argued, 'why can we not have it also with the Allies?'[11]

The argument was set out in an especially clear-cut way by General V. F. Novitskii, in a work written in 1922, an English version of which was published in 1924 (*Russia and the Allies in the Great War*), as part of the Soviets' counter-propaganda to Western claims for compensation for losses allegedly due to the Bolshevik Revolution. The general answered the charge that the Brest-Litovsk peace, through enabling Germany to transfer troops from Russia to France, had threatened disaster to the French and British, by asserting (pp. 35–6) that

> the troops arriving from Russia could hardly increase to any extent the military power of Germany on the Western front because, in the majority of cases, they had lost a large part of their fighting power and were at breaking point . . . . This leads us to infer that if the transport of the German troops from the Eastern to the Western front gave a certain numerical superiority to the armies fighting against the Allies, the importance of this material difference was largely compensated by the inferior quality of these already disaffected reinforcements. Now, if one takes into consideration the fact that the definite triumph of the Allies over Germany was due not to their military superiority, not to the tactical operations, nor in the main to the success of their arms, but to the dissolution of the German army, . . . one cannot but infer that the transport of the German army from the East to the West was more useful to the Allies than to Germany. It was this very Russian Revolution on which the Allies wished to throw the whole of the responsibility for the weakening of the coalition – a weakening more apparent than real – which passed over the Russian frontier and spread throughout Germany, making it possible for the Allies to rout with ease their one-time powerful enemy.

Here, then, we have the schema in its starkest form. Far from helping the German imperialists to reach the brink of victory in the

West, the Bolsheviks, by enabling them to transfer politically-infected troops to that front, actually made possible the victory of the Allies. This view of the history of the year 1918 is endorsed by such important Soviet spokesmen as A. A. Gromyko and B. N. Ponomarev, in the *History of Soviet Foreign Policy* published under their editorship in 1981, where they write that Brest-Litovsk 'was an important contribution by the Soviet state to the speedy ending of the world war' (vol. I, p. 96). The only high-level repudiation of it – and this merely implicit – which is known to me was offered by Stalin in his speech of 3 July 1941, when he said that 'Kaiser Wilhelm's German army in the period of the first imperialist war . . . was finally smashed by the Anglo-French forces' (*On the Great Patriotic War* [1943], p. 5). But the circumstances in which that speech was made were rather special . . .[12]

2 Russia's Defection and the Western Front

In their treatment of the matter of the transfer of German troops from East to West at the end of 1917 and the beginning of 1918, Soviet writers follow two not entirely compatible lines: on the one hand, the Bolsheviks, they say, hindered this transfer, while, on the other, in so far as it occurred, it was a Good Thing. What were the circumstances? The German High Command had at that time grave need of extra troops on the Western Front. After their losses in the Somme battle in 1916 they had been unable to launch any large-scale offensive in France, that is, on the front they knew to be the decisive one, and concentrated their efforts instead against Russia, Romania and Italy, while hoping (vainly) for big results from the U-boat campaign.[1] America's entry into the war then brought the threat that large fresh armies from across the Atlantic would soon join the tired French and British. The Bolshevik revolution and its peace initiative came at the right moment for Germany. When General Hoffmann, chief of staff of the Germans' northern army group on the Russian front, learnt of the Bolsheviks' request for an armistice, he telephoned the news to Ludendorff, who asked: 'Is it possible to negotiate with these people?' Hoffmann replied: 'Yes, it is possible to negotiate with them. Your Excellency needs troops, and this is the quickest way to get them.'[2] The Bolsheviks were trying to bring about a general conclusion of peace and did not wish to appear in the eyes of the people in the Allied countries as helpmates of Germany. They therefore sought to insist that during the period of the armistice no troops should be moved from Russia to the West. Gromyko and Ponomarev (1981, p. 37) claim that the Germans agreed to this proviso: 'Soviet diplomacy had achieved a major trump: the Germans gave way on one of the most important questions – they agreed not to transfer troops from the Eastern to the Western Front.' D. V. Verzhkovskii and V. F. Lyakhov, in *Pervaya mirovaya voina* (1964), complain (p. 8):

> The French General René Tournès asserts[3] that the October Revolution in Russia and the Bolsheviks' struggle for peace helped Germany by freeing her forces in the East. He keeps silent

> about the fact that, under the conditions of the armistice German troops were not to be transferred from the Russian front to the West. . . .

A. O. Chubaryan, in *Brestskii mir* (1964), writes (p. 68) that Germany was obliged to agree to the Soviet condition about no transfers of troops – but then, on the next page, quotes the actual terms of the armistice, which said no transfers should take place 'except those already ordered'. The German historian W. Steglich, in *Die Friedenspolitik der Mittelmächte, 1917–1918*, comments on the significance of that escape-clause:

> Since the German army command had taken the precaution during the armistice negotiations of ordering the transfer of more than one-third of the divisions stationed in the east, the provision merely enabled the Russians to save face *vis-à-vis* their allies: in practical terms it was without significance.[4]

According to John Terraine, *To Win A War* (1978; p. 37), there were 150 German divisions on the Western Front at the beginning of November 1917, but by the end of the year their number had increased to 171. Further transfers between that date and 18 March 1918, a few days before the great offensive began, brought the total to 192. Besides men, some 5000 guns were transferred. Nor must one overlook the 'qualitative' point made by Martin Middlebrook, in *The Kaiser's Battle* (1978, p. 40), that 'the failure of Russia at the end of 1917 had released not only large German forces for use in the West but also some of the finest talent in German generalship'. When the British Fifth Army was forced to fall back in March 1918, this was due to the attack launched by the German Eighteenth Army under the leadership of General Oskar von Hutier, the victor of Riga, who had brought with him his famous artillery specialist, Lieutenant-Colonel Bruchmüller, nicknamed 'Durchbruchmüller'.[5]

The Soviets' semi-official *Illustrated History of the Russian Revolution* (1928), by E. Astrov and others,[6] dealt thus with the question of troop-transfers: one of the concerns of the Soviet delegation at Brest-Litovsk was, it appears, 'not to weaken the military situation on the "Allied" front', and so

> the delegation endeavoured, with every means in their power, to prevent the transference of troops from the Eastern to the Western front of the Entente (at that time no-one understood that this transference of the troops of the Quadruple Alliance,

> which from a military point of view had already been demoralised and exposed to revolutionary propaganda, would form one of the most essential causes of the defeat of German and Austro-Hungarian imperialism).

A point was established in the armistice forbidding transfers: 'however, troops were transferred in spite of the ban, as was to be expected, but this, as has been said above, led rather to the defeat of the imperialists of the Quadruple Alliance than to their salvation' (p. 498).

But how did those 'demoralised' German soldiers actually conduct themselves when they arrived on the Western Front and, on 21 March 1918, were hurled into the biggest military operation the world had seen up to that time? As is well known – at least, in the West – they fought bravely and well, and came close to achieving the aims set by their commanders: to separate the British and French armies, drive the British into the Channel, capture Paris, and end the war before sufficient American troops could enter the battle. The offensive in France was called by the Germans the *Friedensturm*, the attack that would bring about a general peace. Having succeeded in the East, now, it was hoped, Germany would enjoy similar success in the West. 'Now Germany could do what it had wanted to do almost four years earlier: break the enemy's determination to fight, divide the Allies, throw the one into the sea and seize the other's capital. Then would be the time to make peace, a peace that was worth the fight.'[7] General von Kuhl wrote, in his contribution to the post-war German official inquiry into the causes of the defeat: 'Those who saw the freshness and cheerfulness of the troops in the 1918 offensive must have preserved an unforgettable impression'.[8] Ernst Jünger, who participated in the offensive, describes the mood of German soldiers as they listened to the artillery barrage which prepared the onslaught on 21 March:

> Men were running along the trench and shouting delightedly in each other's ears. Infantry and artillery, engineers and signallers, Prussians and Bavarians, officers and men, were all alike in transports over this elemental expression of German power and were burning with impatience for 9.40, when we were to advance to the attack.[9]

A British military historian confirms this impression of the Germans' keenness to fight at the outset of the great offensive:

> After all the miseries of trench warfare there is no doubt that the average German soldier was prepared to go into this battle willingly, if only to force a result one way or the other and get the war over, although those responsible for the training and morale of the German soldiers had done their work well and few men expected anything but success.[10]

General Groener, recalling that time in the less happy situation of late August, said in a talk to army press officers in Kiev: 'There was then a tremendous outburst of enthusiasm in Germany, similar to what we had experienced during the advance through Belgium in 1914.'[11] An officer of the British Army captured at the beginning of the offensive was held prisoner in Cologne. He spoke German and, until July, found that every German he talked with 'was absolutely convinced that the war was won, and the surrender of Paris only a matter of weeks'.[12] And, indeed, the German army and people had good reason for their initial confidence. A shrewd politician, Gustav Stresemann, could write, so late as 15 June, on the occasion of the Kaiser's birthday: 'Never have we had such grounds as now to believe in victory for Germany.'[13] It showed quite exceptional perspicacity on the part of Prince Rupprecht of Bavaria, commander of the Germans' Northern Army Group in France, when he wrote to Reich Chancellor Hertling on 1 June that decisive victory was no longer within Germany's reach and they should try and make peace while their army still stood on foreign soil.[14]

The Allied forces suffered heavy casualties between March and June – 418 000 British, 433 000 French[15] – and the Germans got to within 40 miles of Paris. Major Lloyd Griscom, the American liaison officer at French GHQ, records that 'Paris seemed almost deserted the evening of June 9th: a million people were said to have fled', and Pétain's chief of staff was declaring, 'with wild gesticulations': 'All is lost! Nothing can save Paris! Nothing!'[16] At an earlier stage of this highly critical period, on 11 April, even in the less volatile British camp, Haig had considered it necessary to issue an unusually frank and grave appeal to the hard-pressed British troops:

> Many amongst us now are tired. To those I would say that victory will belong to the side which holds out longest . . . . There is no other course open to us but to fight it out. Every position must be

> held to the last man: there must be no retirement. With our backs to the wall, and believing in the justice of our cause, each one of us must fight on to the end. The safety of our homes and the freedom of mankind alike depend on the conduct of each one of us at this critical moment.[17]

This, then, was the reality of the effect of the Bolshevik Revolution and its peace policy upon the conduct of the war. Whatever may be thought of the realism or otherwise of their advocacy of 'revolutionary war', the Russian 'Left' Communists were certainly right when they pointed out that the signing of the Brest-Litovsk treaty would strengthen 'defencist' tendencies in all the warring countries. In Germany the imperialists would now be able to promise the workers peace and bread through imperialist victory, and also frighten them with the prospect of suffering, should they allow their country to be defeated, a fate similar to that which had fallen upon Russia.[18] Rosa Luxemburg commented that the Bolsheviks 'did not take account of the fact that the capitulation of Russia at Brest-Litovsk meant an enormous strengthening of pan-German policy and thus a lessening of the chances for a revolutionary rising in Germany'.[19] After the armistice, Herman Bernstein, of the *New York Herald*, testifying on 18 February 1919 before the same US Senate Committee which heard from Williams, Price and Keddie, said: 'Those who are inclined to praise the Bolsheviks on the ground that they brought about a revolution in Germany do not face the facts squarely. The German revolution came not because of the Bolsheviks but in spite of them. In fact, they retarded the German revolution.'[20]

Had not Trotsky himself warned in 1914 that Russian Socialists attracted by the notion of 'defeatism' ought not to 'entertain the idea of purchasing the doubtful liberation of Russia by the certain destruction of the liberty of Belgium and France, and – what is more important still – thereby inoculating the German and Austrian proletariat with the virus of imperialism'?[21]

3 February 1918 in Russia

In February 1918 the German 'workers in uniform', well and truly inoculated with the virus of imperialism by their victory over post-Tsarist Russia, as Trotsky had foreseen, proceeded to confirm his further prophecy that, if revolution came to Russia in circumstances of military defeat, 'then the bayonets of the Hohenzollern armies would be turned on the revolution'.[1] But to confirm that prophecy only to a limited extent: the limitation (of vital importance) being due to a third factor present. The rulers of Imperial Germany did not like Bolshevism and would have preferred to see a different sort of regime installed in Russia. They humiliated and robbed Bolshevik-ruled Russia. But they stopped short – for the time being – of actually overthrowing the Bolsheviks, because the latter were the only political group in Russia ready to accept and more or less to comply with their peace terms. The Germans' preoccupation with the Western Front meant that they were willing, temporarily, to tolerate 'the revolution', at least within restricted territorial limits. This was the basis for Lenin's subtle policy in the period of the Brest-Litovsk negotiations. Given that any attempt at waging a 'revolutionary war' against German imperialism would, as he saw it, result only in the downfall of the Soviet Government, one had to be ready to make any concession demanded by the Germans, to 'appease' them in every way – on the sole condition that they refrained from intervening against the Bolsheviks in Petrograd, Moscow and the adjacent territories, roughly corresponding to medieval Muscovy.

It is worth while dwelling a little on the circumstances in which the advance of the German forces into Russia, after Trotsky's famous 'no peace, no war' declaration, came to an end and the treaty of Brest-Litovsk was signed, because some Soviet writers have the cheek to suggest that it was the Soviet forces' resistance that brought the Germans back to the conference table. Thus, Yu. Korablev, in his article in *Voenno-istoricheskii zhurnal*, no. 1 of 1968 (p. 28), gives the uninformed reader the impression that the resistance compelled the Germans to make peace; in order to do this he has, of course, to conceal the fact that the final peace terms were worse for Russia than those offered before that episode. E. P. Putyrskii, in *Boevoi Petrograd v 1918 godu* (pp. 52–3) similarly says that the resistance forced the Germans to halt their advance on Petrograd. Comparable passages are found in the *Istoriya grazhdanskoi voiny*, vol. 3 (p. 117), in N. N. Azovtsev *et al.*'s *Krakh pervogo nashestviya imperialistov na stranu Sovetov* (1973, p. 78), and in at least two of the articles in the 1983 encyclopaedia of the Civil War and intervention edited by S. S. Khromov (pp. 148 and 185). In one of these a totally false notion is conveyed of the burden of Lenin's article on the week 18–24 February 1918, entitled 'A Painful but Necessary Lesson'. The more honest Soviet historians show embarrassed awareness that this distortion of Lenin is committed by their colleagues: thus, Colonel S. Lipitskii, in a book review in *Voenno-istoricheskii zhurnal* no. 1 of 1982 remarks (p. 80) that the important Lenin article mentioned is sometimes 'subjected to arbitrary interpretations'. In 'A Painful but Necessary Lesson' Lenin was quite categoric:

> There have been the painful and humiliating reports of regiments refusing to retain their positions, of refusal to defend even the Narva Line, and of disobedience to the order to destroy everything in the event of a retreat, not to mention the running away, the chaos, ineptitude, helplessness and slovenliness.[2]

Not a word does Lenin utter in this article about any heroic defence that might have forced the Germans to change their plans. That there certainly were isolated instances of heroism by small Red volunteer groups on the approaches to Petrograd is well attested, but what is also clear is that these actions were on a very limited scale and had little if any effect on General Hoffmann's operation.

One contemporary observer, the French diplomat Louis de Robien, noted in his diary for 25 February 1918 that when, on receipt of the news that the Germans had taken Pskov, the Petrograd Soviet appealed for volunteers to defend the city, 'at the Charlier factory only 19 out of 4000 workmen volunteered, in spite of sirens and proclamations', and claims that the situation was the same at other factories.[3] Another, the French journalist 'C. Anet' (J. Schoffer) recorded on 24 February: 'It is claimed that 3000 workers at the Vulcan factory have joined up. I cannot verify those figures, but for a factory which I do know I have the exact number of volunteers: out of 1800 workers there were 14.'[4] One of the most honest of the Soviet historians of this episode, A. L. Fraiman, debunks the allegation made by A. E. Antonov (perhaps the *least* honest) in his *Boevoi vosemnadtsatyi god* (1961, p. 23) that on 23

February *35 000* workers signed up for the Red Army, a statement which, Fraiman coldly comments, 'is not supported by any evidence and is without foundation'.[5] Fraiman says that the records show that no more than 3000 volunteers had enlisted by the evening of 24 February, and the *total* number obtained between 19 February and 6 March did not exceed 38 000.[6] In his speech on 7 March to the 7th Party Congress, Sverdlov said that the defence problem in February had been not merely that the peasants would not fight – neither would the mass of the workers. ('I am not talking about the revolutionary upper strata of the proletariat, but of the masses.') If the Bolsheviks were to throw their best units into battle against the Germans (as some were still advocating they should), it would mean suicide, both physical and political. Those units must inevitably consist of the people without whom the October Revolution would have been unthinkable, and who were still indispensable if Bolshevik power was to survive. By sending those units to perish they would be cutting off the branch on which they sat. Reporting on the Congress to the activists of the Nizhegorod Party organisation on 23 March he emphasised that the Soviet Government had lacked the forces to check the German offensive, even temporarily. True, they had assembled a few thousand volunteers in Petrograd, but these were all outstanding Party members. The masses did *not* turn up to volunteer, and the shrewdest of the Bolshevik leaders saw that if they carried on fighting they would only succeed in losing their best people, and then have to accept the German terms anyway.[7]

It should, in all fairness, be mentioned that the Left SR, Steinberg, who was then a member of the Soviet Government and an advocate of 'revolutionary war', claimed in his *Als ich Volkskommissar war* (1929, p. 227 seq.) that Lenin deliberately painted a gloomy picture of the military position, playing down the possibilities of resistance.[8] Fraiman points out that the way in which the story of February 1918 was always told in Stalin's time, as though there had been 'real possibilities for a quick victory over the enemy', gave retrospective support to the line of the 'revolutionary war' faction who opposed Lenin! (Fraiman [1961], pp. 10–12). He also notes that, far from exaggerating the setbacks at the front, Lenin gave credence to a false report that Pskov had been recaptured by the Red forces (and mentions that this pseudo-fact, though quickly discredited at the time, has been reproduced as truth by subsequent Soviet historians, notably R. N. Mordvinov and N. Kuzmin).[9]

In so far as the German advance in February–March 1918 was

obstructed at all, a great deal of the credit belongs to the Allied (especially French) officers who came to the aid of the Soviet Government at this most difficult moment. At the meeting of the Bolshevik Party's Central Committee on 22 February, Trotsky reported that the French and British had offered help, and read a note from the French military mission. As is well-known, Lenin backed the view of that section of the (almost evenly divided) committee who favoured 'taking weapons from the imperialist robbers'.[10] The devoted efforts of the Allied officers were largely frustrated by lack of co-operation from the forces supposedly defending 'Soviet power'. When Dvinsk fell, the Germans acquired its arsenal, intact, with 2000 guns. Lieutenant de Lubersac, of the French military mission (the officer mentioned by Lenin in his *Letter to American Workers*[11]), who stayed there until the last minute, had persuaded the local Reds to agree to blow up the citadel, but they failed to do this: he himself managed to destroy the stocks of petrol and forage.[12] Lindley, the British Chargé d'Affaires, reported to the Foreign Office on 25 February that the Germans had taken Pskov 'with 150 men' and had also interrupted Petrograd's rail link with Reval, so that 'two of our four officers sent there last night at the request of the Russians, with a demolition party, are returning'.[13] Captain Cromie, the British naval attaché, recalling the February episode in a report on 2 May to Admiral Phillimore, wrote of how 'it was a staggering blow to the country to see how fast their men ran, leaving rolling-stock and bridges intact behind them, even after we had prepared some of the latter for destruction'.[14]

Altogether, the experience of February–March 1918 showed the impossibility of effective resistance to the Germans being offered by Soviet Russia. The most zealous and skilful of Anglo-French demolition and evacuation experts, in however large numbers, could not substitute for a large body of reliable, disciplined soldiers, adequate to confront such a force as Germany's army on the Eastern Front still constituted at this stage, even though its depletion for service in the West was already well-advanced.[15]

This brings us to the question of how to appreciate the negotiations that went on, *after* the signing of the peace treaty, between the Soviet Government (usually in the person of Trotsky) and representatives of the Allied powers, with a view to assistance being given by the latter for building the Red Army.

4 Brest-Litovsk and After

The fate of Russia in the months following Brest-Litovsk depended on the outcome of a tense triangular relationship between the Allies, the Germans and the Bolsheviks. The Allies' concern was to restore the Eastern Front, if possible, or at least to minimise the advantages gained by the Germans from their victory over Russia. For the Germans what mattered was to keep Russia out of the war and to exploit the country's weakness (and especially that of its new government) to the utmost. What mattered to the Bolsheviks was, first and foremost, to stay in power and, secondly, to promote their international revolutionary objectives, in so far as these were compatible with staying in power.

The most immediate preoccupation of the Allies after Brest-Litovsk was with the fate of the large quantities of military supplies which had been sent to Russia while she was still in the war, and which, for lack of transport facilities and other reasons, had piled up in the ports of Murmansk and Archangel (and, in the Far East, at Vladivostok). These must not be allowed to disappear into the interior, where, all too probably, they would fall into the hands of the Germans.[1] For this reason a small British force was landed at Murmansk at the moment when it seemed that the Germans were about to occupy Petrograd, at the other end of the Murman Railway, which had been built during the war for the very purpose of conveying these supplies from the northern port to the front against Germany. At first the British at Murmansk enjoyed the co-operation of the local Bolsheviks. On 1 March, when it was thought by the Bolshevik Government that the Germans were going to refuse to halt their offensive and allow the Bolsheviks to sign a peace treaty, Trotsky ordered the Murmansk Soviet to 'accept any and all assistance from the Allied missions and use every means to obstruct the advance of the plunderers'.[2]

The danger to the stores at Murmansk was not the only cause for anxiety to the Allies in that quarter. When the Germans intervened in the Finnish Civil War the possibility arose that, either directly or through their 'White' Finnish allies, they would get control of Pechenga (Petsamo), to the west of Murmansk, and establish there a submarine base from which to prey on Allied shipping in the North Atlantic. British troops and 'Red' Finns found themselves fighting side by side against the German-backed 'White' Finns when the latter advanced on Pechenga (and on the Murman Railway at Kandalaksha). Worried about how the Germans would view this situation, Foreign Affairs Commissar Chicherin requested that the British Foreign Office warn the British commander up there 'to let as little news from Murmansk get out to the outside world both in Russia and abroad as possible'.[3] A few days later, Lockhart was able to report on a talk with the Finnish Communist leader Tokoi about the military co-operation between the British and the 'Red' Finns, in which Tokoi reported that 'Lenin had informed him he would look through his fingers at any action England took at Murmansk to help the Finns'.[4] That was in early May. So late as 18 May the Admiralty could tell the British commander at Murmansk that, according to Lockhart, the

> Moscow authorities do not wish us to withdraw, although they are compelled by [the] German attitude to make formal protest against our remaining. It is realised that [the] Central [Soviet] Government must be considerably embarrassed at [the] present time, as they know [the] Germans have [the] necessary power to carry out their threats, whilst [the] Allies are not yet ready to intervene.[5]

And, six days after that, Trotsky told Lockhart that the naval experts in the service of the Soviet Government were strongly in favour of the Allies remaining at Murmansk, since, if they withdrew, Russia would risk being cut off completely from the rest of Europe except through outlets controlled directly or indirectly by the Germans.[6]

But the attitude of the Soviet Government towards the Allies was already beginning to change, under pressure from Germany. On 22 May Chicherin found it necessary to warn the Murmansk Soviet that, 'in view of the general political situation, any appeal to the British for help is quite impermissible', and even if the British were fighting the White Finns, 'we must not join them as allies, and we shall protest against their actions on our territory'.[7] Alert to the signs of change, E. H. Carr, then working at the Foreign Office, wrote in a minute dated 27 May that the Soviet Government was 'obviously trying to play a double game over the Murman question and keep in with both sides. The only moral is that our forces in the north should be made as strong as possible.'[8]

Between March and May of 1918 there were other dealings too

between the Allies and the Bolsheviks, inspired by the concern of the former to frustrate Germany's aims. The French Government sent instructions to General Niessel, head of their military mission in Russia, on 8 and 11 March, to encourage Soviet resistance to Germany in any way possible, so that when, on 20 March, Trotsky formally requested their co-operation in rebuilding the Russian Army, General Lavergne, who had by then replaced Niessel, responded favourably, and by the beginning of April French officers were ready to assume advisory functions in the Red Army.[9] On 3 April Litvinov, semi-officially representing the Soviet Government in London, asked his Foreign Office contact Rex Leeper if he could be given facilities to train Russians resident in Britain for service in the Red Army. He had two officers of the old army available for this work (Captains Oshmyanskii and Semyonov), and the soldiers would be sent in 'through northern ports'. The British War Office recommended that, while Litvinov should certainly not be allowed to train soldiers in Britain, he should be given facilities to despatch to Russia such recruits as he was able to raise.[10]

By the middle of April, however, it had become apparent to the Allied authorities that the army they were being asked to help into being was one so constructed and controlled as to serve the purpose of civil war rather than national defence – 'a sort of Praetorian Guard' for the Soviet regime, as a Political Intelligence Department memorandum put it (10 April).[11] France's consul-general in Moscow, Grenard, had talks in early April with the Russian monarchist group around E. N. Trubetskoi, and they warned him that not only would the Red Army not fight Germany but, if the Allies continued to help build it, the anti-Bolshevik elements would, in despair, turn to Germany for support, so that, in the end, France would have gained nothing and lost something (M. J. Carley, *Revolution and Intervention: The French Government and the Russian Civil War, 1917–1919* [1983], p. 57.) M. N. Pokrovskii, writing in 1927, admitted that an attempt had been made in 1918 to deceive the Allies regarding the Bolsheviks' intention to stand up to German aggression:

> We talked with this motley crowd [that is, the diplomatic and military representatives of the Allies], hoping to squeeze out of them those things which the newly-created workers' republic frantically needed, for the future, the immediate future, to carry on the desperate struggle with the entire bourgeois world . . . Lenin was squinting his eyes cunningly and preparing war not

> against any particular imperialism but against imperialism in general.[12]

Even if the Allies and the Bolsheviks had found a basis for agreement on aid by the former to reconstitute a Russian army owing allegiance to the latter, the process would have taken months to produce results of any significance in the war with Germany. What was urgently needed, from the Allied point of view, was the presence on Russian soil, confronting the Germans, of a large body of well-trained, well-equipped soldiers. In a telegram to Lockhart dated 8 April, Balfour noted that Trotsky seemed to be realising that Russia could not put up any serious resistance to Germany 'for many months to come', and so was ready to accept the necessity of Allied intervention coming from the Far East. However, Trotsky had specified that this must take the form of an expeditionary force 'in which American troops formed the main nucleus'. Balfour supposed that Trotsky had

> not reflected on the only way in which [intervention] could be effected. Owing entirely to Russian defection, Germany's whole strength can now be exerted on the Western front. The Western powers, therefore, including America, have to concentrate on that front all their troops not already engaged elsewhere. The only power which has forces available for a Far Eastern campaign is therefore Japan . . . .[13]

In their desperation at this moment when Germany looked to be on the point of breaking through finally in the West, the leaders of Britain and France appear seriously to have imagined that their 'sleeping-partner' ally, Japan, would be prepared not merely to occupy Eastern Siberia up to Lake Baikal (something the Japanese would be quite willing to do, for reasons that had no connection with the world war) but to push on westward until they clashed with the Germans. At the time, indeed, the idea did not seem so fantastic to an observer like Captain Jacques Sadoul, of the French Embassy, soon to become a keen pro-Bolshevik. In a letter of 3 May he contemplated a scenario in which the small Allied forces landed in North Russia would link up with several Japanese army corps in the Urals–Volga region: 'But if the hoped-for success is to crown our efforts, it would seem to be essential that Japan commit herself thoroughly [*s'engage à fond*].'[14] In rejecting with gestures of horror the prospect of *Japanese* intervention, the Bolshevik leaders were on a good wicket, in that (without saying this in so many words) they could appeal to the patriotic feelings of many Russians who were still sore from the defeat inflicted on their country by Japan in 1905. (In 1905, of course, the Bolsheviks had taken a 'defeatist' line, and one may presume that even Stalin would, in 1918, have been sickened by the speech he was to make on 2 September 1945, on the occasion of Japan's surrender at the end of the Second World War, when he claimed that 'for forty years have we, men of the older generation, waited for this day'). An even deeper reservoir of Russian gut-feeling against yellow men could be drawn upon: the bitter memory of 'the Mongol yoke' (though this did not in the least inhibit the Bolsheviks from making extensive use of Chinese and Koreans in the Red Army and the Cheka during the Civil War). Nevertheless, after the game with the Allies was over, and it was necessary to justify the more consistent 'German orientation' adopted by the Soviet Government from June onward, Trotsky saw fit to provide a sort of 'Marxist' (Menshevik?) explanation of the Bolsheviks' rejection of military aid from Japan:

> If our Soviet Republic should be . . . forced to choose between German and Japanese troops, I would say . . . better the German army than the Japanese, because the German is more cultured, the people are more educated, and there are more workers, and awakening is possible; whereas the Japanese are an alien people, we do not know their language, the working class is less conscious, much time must pass before a revolution will develop on Japanese soil. Japanese rule is more bitter, more terrible than the rule of the Germans.[15]

One wonders what the workers and peasants in the Ukraine, under the German jackboot, thought of this academic comparison between German rule and another, hypothetical variety, to the advantage of the former. As for the revolutionary possibilities of different countries, who, before 1917, expected a socialist revolution in Russia sooner than one in Germany? And (the main consideration, surely?), was not the German army holding positions within easy striking distance of Petrograd and Moscow, whereas the Japanese were far away and likely to remain so?

At this point it is appropriate to look carefully at the question of Lenin's attitude towards the Allies and their anti-German moves in Russia. In January 1918, in his 'Theses on the question of a separate peace', he had flatly opposed, not merely renewal of the alliance with Britain and France, but even such independent action by Soviet Russia as would be of help to them.

> A revolutionary war [against Germany] at the present juncture would, objectively speaking, make us agents of Anglo-French imperialism by providing it with forces which would promote its aims . . . . Even if we did not take a single kopek from the Anglo-French, we nevertheless would be helping them, objectively speaking, by diverting part of the German army. From that point of view, in neither case would we be escaping some sort of imperialist bond . . . . We always discountenanced victory over an alien imperialism, victory attained in formal or actual alliance with a 'friendly' imperialism, as a method impermissible in principle and generally wrong.[16]

When the Germans resumed their offensive, he could still write, on 21 February, about Allied offers of help: 'The Anglo-French bourgeoisie are setting a trap for us: please be kind enough to go and fight *now*, our gain will be magnificent.'[17] Next day, however, as the menace grew, he modified his attitude, as is shown in his famous message to the 22 February meeting of the Bolshevik Party's Central Committee: 'Please include my vote *in favour* of getting potatoes [*sic*] and arms from the bandits of Anglo-French imperialism.'[18] And in his article 'The Itch', written on that same day, he reminded his readers that 'the North Americans in their war of liberation against England at the end of the 18th Century got help from Spain and France, who were her competitors and just as much colonial robbers as England'.[19] (Here he was arguing against those elements in his party who, with sublime unrealism, were advocating a 'revolutionary war' against Germany while at the same time refusing to accept help in such a war from Germany's imperialist rivals.)

Once, however, it had become clear that the Germans were *not* going to force the Bolsheviks to fight, but would let them off the hook provided they signed the 'Tilsit peace' dictated to them, Lenin reverted to his 'January' position. He was firm for signing the treaty, and for ratifying it. Here, something has to be said concerning Raymond Robins' story about the note Trotsky gave him on 5 March, for transmission to the United States Government, asking what help the Soviet Government could expect from that quarter in the event that it refused to ratify the Brest-Litovsk treaty and then had to face renewed war with Germany.[20] Robins implies that it was only when (and because) no reply was received in time to this request that Lenin recommended to the Congress of Soviets that they ratify the treaty. That ratification was indeed in doubt, so far as Lenin was concerned, has been taken as fact, on Robins' say-so, by a number of Western historians. Yet it seems unlikely to say the least, that the Lenin who was arguing strongly on 23 February that Russia was in no state to fight Germany, because the peasants did not want war, would have thought the situation substantially different less than a month later, merely on the offchance that the USA might agree to send some instructors and equipment. On 1 March he expressed the view that, while the infant Red Army was 'undoubtedly splendid fighting material', this was 'raw unfinished material. In order that it may not become cannon-fodder for the German guns, it must be trained and disciplined.'[21] And if the peace treaty were not ratified without delay, the Germans could not be expected to stand idly by while that process reached completion. The resolution of the special Party Congress held on 6–8 March, in favour of ratification, made, as Kennan points out, 'no mention whatsoever of Allied aid as a factor in the problem, and frankly placed the entire hope for the survival and further success of Soviet power on the spread of revolution to the Western countries generally.'[22] Why was Robins (who, of course, did not know about this Party Congress resolution, which was kept secret until after ratification had gone through) still expecting something different to happen right down to the moment, on 11 March, when the Congress of Soviets ratified the treaty? Kennan again:

> It is difficult to understand . . . how it was possible . . . to believe that there was a serious possibility that the Soviet Government might invite the Allies in . . . [Robins and Lockhart] were unquestionably diverted and misled by Trotsky's statements, which reflected partly his greater pessimism (as compared with Lenin) over the chances for prolonging the breathing-space, and partly, no doubt, his desire to exploit Allied interest as a means of discouraging Japanese intervention.[23]

Another possible motive for Trotsky's encouraging – and Lenin's not too brutally discouraging – the illusions of Robins and Lockhart is suggested by Ulam. Many Bolsheviks expected that the capitalists of the Allied countries and those of the Central Powers would be strongly inclined, 'in accordance with class interests', to cease their mutual strife and gang up against Soviet Russia, the firebrand of world revolution, and so it was vital to counter that tendency by dangling before the Allies the prospect that Soviet Russia might not prove so world-revolutionary as to refuse an alliance with one group of imperialists against the other.[24]

Let us not leave Raymond Robins without a glance at the comments on his efforts made by the British General Knox and by a Soviet historian. Knox wrote, in a memorandum of 18 March, circulated to the War Cabinet, that Robins 'is a fanatic with the temperament of a hero-worshipping schoolgirl, and while without the mental equipment or the experience to enable him to advise on policy, he is a dangerous companion for anyone as impressionable as Lockhart'.[25] A. O. Chubaryan, one of the leading Soviet authorities on this period, takes quite a different view of the 'Robins initiative' from that of Western writers who go along with Robins in using its failure as an 'excuse' for Soviet Russia's ratification of the peace treaty. 'In reality,' Chubaryan insists,

> Lenin was not preparing to break off negotiations [with Germany] even if aid were to be received from the Allies . . . . He in no way linked the sending of the note [to the US Government] with the question of ratification of the Brest peace. Lenin agreed to the note because he was sympathetic to the actions and intentions of Robins. In addition, Lenin had no objection to sounding out the position of American ruling circles.[26]

This Soviet writer draws, as might be expected, a sharp line between the motives of Lenin and those of Trotsky in respect to their dealings with Robins, Lockhart and Sadoul. Trotsky he sees as actually working hand in glove with these agents of the Allies to draw Russia, against her own interests, back into the imperialist war.[27] Where Lenin was merely humouring Robins and making use of him for reconnaissance purposes, Trotsky's conversations with Robins and the others were, so to speak, criminally sincere, or so we are led to believe.

At this point we should examine Trotsky's conduct in relation to the Allies in the first five months of 1918. To what extent *was* he sincere in his dealings with Lockhart, Robins and Sadoul? Was he really following a policy of his own, different from Lenin's? Or was there a cunning 'division of labour' operating here?

Present-day Soviet historians have no doubt that Trotsky acted in this period virtually as an agent of the Allies in their endeavour to get Russia back into the war with Germany. Chubaryan says that 'Trotsky's actions corresponded fully to his political line directed towards rupture of the peace with Germany'.[28] O. F. Solovyov, writing of the activities of Lockhart, Robins and Sadoul aimed at preventing the conclusion of peace, says that 'these representatives of the Allies established, above all, close relations with Trotsky, so as to use him in the interests of the Entente'.[29] Count Mirbach, the German ambassador in Moscow appointed after Brest-Litovsk, saw Trotsky in the same light, even so late as 28 May, when he wrote in an official despatch: 'He [Trotsky] can now plainly be characterised as the spokesman of a pro-Entente orientation within the Council of People's Commissars.'[30] The British Consul in Moscow, Oliver Wardrop, reported on 2 April that he had information to the effect that there was a definite difference of opinion on foreign policy between Lenin and Trotsky – that the latter wished, by immediate action, to provoke Germany to adopt an aggressive policy towards Russia, in the belief that the German Social-Democrats would then rebel against their government.[31] Sadoul, in a letter of 12 April, reported that the French officers working with the Red Army staff were impressed by Trotsky's friendly attitude: 'All doors were wide open to them, and all sources of information put at their disposal.'[32] This picture is confirmed by a recent Soviet historian, who quotes, from the archives, a message of that same date from the Commissar of the Western sector of the 'screens' (the Soviet troops facing the Germans along the demarcation line laid down by the peace treaty), asking whether it was permissible to give information to the French military mission, and Trotsky's affirmative reply.[33]

On the other hand, Trotsky himself (in an explanatory note in volume XVII, part 1, of his works, published in 1925) plays down the implications of his dealings with the French military mission, explaining (p. 673) that, 'on my part, the purpose of these negotiations was to obtain military *matériel*', leaving the reader to deduce whether or not the purpose for which he wanted this *matériel* was the same as that for which the Allies might offer it. Avtonomov, commander of the Red forces in Northern Caucasia, sent in May 1918 one of his officers, Shostak, to Moscow to request that these forces be sent into the Ukraine to strengthen the anti-German struggle there. After a fortnight of fruitless talks, Shostak came to the conclusion that *none* of the People's Commissars seriously intended renewing the conflict with Germany, and that the Allied military missions were being made fools of.[34] General Niessel quotes in his book a letter he wrote during this period: 'I wonder whether Trotsky has not been play-acting in his requests for our help. It was a way of keeping our Embassy and military mission at his beck and call, their presence here enabling the Bolsheviks to maintain the appearance of a government which, even if not formally recognised, at least enjoys some standing.'[35] E. H. Carr minuted on 24 June a message from Lockhart reporting that, despite Trotsky's promises, the military stores at Archangel were being evacuated at an increased rate, so that in another month there would be nothing left: 'This tells us only what we knew before, that Trotsky was simply playing with us over this. The only novelty is that Mr. Lockhart's eyes have been opened.'[36] The fact that Trotsky evidently did not tell Lockhart about the secret Bolshevik Party Congress which, meeting between 6 and 8 March, decided to go for ratification of the peace treaty indicates, as Ullman puts it, that 'the relationship between the two was less open than the British agent believed'.[37] At the US Senate hearings in 1919 Senator Nelson commented, when Robins mentioned that Trotsky had stayed away, 'sulking', from the Congress of Soviets at which the peace treaty was ratified: 'One of the two leaders was for the treaty and the other stood back. Was not that for a purpose, to have an anchor to windward?'[38]

Whatever the truth of the matter regarding possible differences of view or of approach between Lenin and Trotsky, it was Lenin who ultimately decided, and he, at any rate, was well aware of the implications of his government's role as a government not of the Russian people as a whole but of certain sections of the Russian people engaged in civil war against the rest. A renewed war with Germany, however conceived by Bukharin and the other advocates of 'revolutionary war', would all too probably develop – indeed, to be successful, would have to develop – as a *national* war. 'The prospect of Allied assistance did not appeal to him', writes Debo. 'Such aid would bring with it unwanted political advice, and the last thing he wanted was Buchanan, Noulens or Francis whispering in his ear about the delights of a *union sacrée* uniting all parties in a patriotic war against the Germans. . . .'[39] (In 1941–5 Stalin found it necessary to call on the Russian people to fight for the Russia of Dmitri Donskoi, and to make concessions to the Orthodox Church: but by that time the opposition forces that existed in 1918 had been 'liquidated' and an effective apparatus of control established, so that the risk was not so great.)

5 The Great German Offensive

The Soviet Government was not, however, only a government of civil war, it was also a government that saw as its duty – and also as the ultimate condition of its survival – the promoting of revolution throughout the world, and especially in the 'advanced countries'. This meant, in the Bolsheviks' view, under the conditions of the world war then in progress, promoting defeatism in the belligerent countries, France and Britain included. That was a policy hard to reconcile with any sort of friendly arrangement with those states. Litvinov, the Bolsheviks' representative in Britain, told the Labour Party's annual conference in January 1918: 'I would say to the representatives of the British labour, "speed up your peace." '[1] In the *Daily Herald* he wrote: 'The further prolongation of the war must lead to the defeat of the Russian Revolution and to the triumph of militarism and reaction everywhere.' (For any reader who might object that the *immediate* threat was from specifically *German* militarism he had the reassuring message that the Soviets' 'revolutionary propaganda among the German soldiers on the Western front and among prisoners of war is undermining the strength of German autocracy and militarism more effectively than military victories could, and has already provoked a strong peace movement in Germany and Austria.' This was, of course, before the German army's February offensive in Russia.)[2] In the *Woolwich Pioneer* of 8 February Litvinov wrote that 'the Russian proletariat' expected the proletariat of all other countries to start an 'energetic and unflinching struggle for peace'.[3] As well as making general propaganda along these lines, the Bolshevik representative carried on a more specialised activity among and concerning men with a Russian background who were either in the British army or were due to be called up for military service. According to a police informant's report on a talk with Litvinov, 6 February, Litvinov said: 'It will be my business to see that not a single Russian subject is compelled to stay in the British Army, irrespective of whether the unit is at home or abroad.'[4] He wrote formally to Balfour on 13 February protesting against the call-up of Russians in Britain,[5] and told his Foreign Office contact Rex Leeper on 14 February that he wanted proceedings stopped against Russians who had not answered their call-up.[6] The War Cabinet was informed on 22 February that Litvinov was meeting a lot of soldiers 'of Jewish descent' and urging them 'to engage in propaganda in their regiments'.[7]

By that date, however, the Germans' drive towards Petrograd had somewhat confused the issue for the Bolsheviks. A Foreign Office document of 23 February records that 'Mr. Leeper has just informed us that Litvinoff proposes to issue an appeal through the press to all Russians in England to return to Russia to fight a holy revolutionary war against the Germans. Litvinoff is anxious to know whether he would have the approval of H.M.G. in so doing.' J. D. Gregory thought this a good idea: it would get rid of 'a lot of superfluous Russians' and, 'far more important', it would have 'a salutary effect on Labour here'.[8] However, the Bolsheviks' surrender to Germany deprived the project of practical significance for the immediate future.

When Kamenev and two colleagues arrived in England, on their way, as they hoped, to France, they were interviewed by some Foreign Office representatives, in Litvinov's office, on 27 February. Kamenev explained frankly that his purpose was to promote everywhere revolutions of the kind that Russia had undergone. The British report of this meeting notes that Kamenev was 'not very successful in answering the question addressed to him by Mr. Namier, what would be the effect if such a revolution broke out in one or more of the Entente countries before it broke out in Germany?'[9] Trotsky seems to have been aware of the problem hinted at by Lewis Namier, and in an interview with Lockhart on 27 March assured him that 'Litvinov has been ordered to stop all pacifist propaganda and to conduct himself more tactfully'.[10] (However, a Foreign Office telegram to Lockhart dated 20 April said: 'Although, as far as we are aware, M. Litvinoff has of late abstained from political agitation and propaganda, it is as well that you should know that he has not received the instructions promised by M. Trotsky in this sense.'[11])

After the great German offensive on the Western Front began, on 21 March, and increasingly between then and the turn of the tide in July–August, the mood of the British public was unreceptive to pacifist and defeatist influences, and Litvinov must have discovered that that was so, if he ever made any attempt to resume his activity of January and early February. The British reaction to the great onslaught proved, indeed, to be a terrible disappointment to the German High Command.

> For forty days, from March 21 to the end of April, the main strength of Germany had been ceaselessly devoted to the battery and destruction of the British Army . . . By their stubborn and skilful resistance at every point, by numberless small parties fighting unchronicled till they were blotted out, the British inflicted upon the Germans losses even greater than those they themselves endured, losses which broke the supreme German effort for victory at the outset, and rang the knell of doom in the ears of the overwrought German people. (Winston Churchill, *The World Crisis*, Part 2 [1927], p. 447)

Once the United States had entered the war, 'it had become impossible for the Central Empires to achieve victory, so long as the Allies did not slacken'.[12] Accordingly,

> the overall plan of the Germans in their spring attacks in 1918 was so to weaken the British Expeditionary Force that either the British soldiers would break or their military and political leaders would lose the will to continue playing a major role in the war. It is against this background that the achievements of the Germans on 21 March should be judged.[13]

Ludendorff expressed to Prince Rupprecht the hope that, as a result of the great offensive, a revolution in Paris or London would come to Germany's aid, 'as in Russia'.[14] In his letter of 1 June to Hertling, already mentioned, Rupprecht voiced his doubts about that prospect: Ludendorff, he said, 'was unreasonably relying on one of the Western Powers collapsing as Russia had'.[15] But Hertling, replying to the Bavarian Prince on 5 June, was still hopeful that things would indeed turn out as Ludendorff expected. 'A succession of blows destroying the military might of France and England would finally result in a powerful popular movement directed against those Governments, a movement that, taken together with the existing and increasing pacifist tendencies in both countries, would lead to the opening of peace negotiations . . . .'[16] Princess Blücher, however, an Englishwoman living in Germany during the war, wrote in her diary for 9 April:

> Everything had been staked on their breaking through the enemy's lines, and they have not done so, although they have driven the enemy back . . . Morally, too, the offensive has not made the wished-for impression on the enemy, but, if anything, has put new courage into them. The pacifists in England and France are fewer and have retired into the background.[17]

The Princess, like the Prince, saw the situation more clearly than the politician. Ironically, the very circumstance that had made possible the great offensive in France contributed to prevent its success.

> The victim [at Brest-Litovsk] was to drag down the oppressor. For it was the Brest-Litovsk negotiations . . . which first taught an astounded world the inner meaning of a 'German peace'.[18]

> Looked at in the light of Brest-Litovsk, the future of Western Europe, in case of a German victory, was a dismal one indeed. If only the representatives of the German people had shown that they were not in accord with their government's annexationist policy! But quite the opposite happened.[19]

> In the first imperialist peace the peoples of the world thought they saw *the first German peace* . . . The disgraceful peace imposed upon Russia caused fresh enthusiasm for the war among the Allied and neutral peoples. All thoughts of negotiation now went by the board: the idea of a compromise peace, which had been in the air up till then, simply vanished.[20]

> Even the Socialists must now recognise, Clemenceau observed grimly, that to negotiate a peace with Germany was for the lamb to lie down with the lion. The Russians had discovered this at Brest-Litovsk.[21]

The spectacle of the peace terms imposed on Russia (and on Romania by the Treaty of Bucharest) dissolved illusions which had been current in the Allied countries about a possible 'peace of understanding', and stiffened the will to resist.

> It was this renewed spirit of resistance which enabled the civilian population to remain calm in the face of the early disasters which followed the launching of the great German offensive on 21 March 1918, and to retain their confidence throughout that fearful spring and early summer until the Allied counter-offensive on 18 July wrested the initiative from the German armies for the last time.[22]

According to Colonel Repington, at the Versailles War Council in February 1918, in reply to 'energetic remonstrances' from the French, Lloyd George said that 'there would be a social revolution if he asked England for more men'. However, 'when the defeat of March compelled the Prime Minister to do his duty there was no social revolution, nor even a whimper'.[23] The militant element among Britain's engineering workers did, indeed, succeed in getting a majority in a ballot against acceptance of the Government's proposal to call up skilled men between the ages of 18 and 25, and on 21 March an unofficial national conference of shop stewards met at Manchester to prepare for strike action. But

> on the day the conference assembled, the Germans launched their last great offensive of the war, and the belated unofficial efforts came to nothing. Strikes and threats of strikes evaporated overnight, militancy was temporarily paralysed by the sudden awareness of military danger. During April 1918 only 3900 working days were lost through strike action, one of the lowest figures of the war.[24]

The Communist Wal Hannington, who was active in this period in promoting strikes, records in his book *Industrial History in Wartime* (1940, p. 64) that 'during the first half of the year 1918 [that is, until July] there was a lull in disputes, during the big German offensive . . .'. Another Communist historian, Tom Wintringham, noted in his *Mutiny* (1936, p. 312) that the effect of the great offensive was actually to reduce expressions of anti-war feeling in the British Army: 'The German attacks on the Western Front in the first half of 1918 made many waverers feel that the war must be continued until safety was assured.' And Anthony Babington, who has studied the judicial consequences of desertion and mutiny in this period, testifies that 'the incidence of military executions in the British Expeditionary Force decreased significantly from the beginning of 1918' (*For the Sake of Example: Capital Courts-Martial 1914–20* [1983], p. 159).

The only allegation of 'Bolshevik-inspired defeatism' in the British Army at the time of the German offensive which is known to me is a statement made by Lieutenant-Commander Sir Warden Chilcott, the Conservative candidate for Liverpool (Walton) during the 1924 general election. In the *Liverpool Post* of 21 October of that year he claimed that subversive propaganda had contributed to the retreat of the British Fifth Army in 1918. The story received nation-wide coverage in the *Daily Express* of 24 October, under the headline: 'Sedition in Army: General's War Charges'. Chilcott gave as his source Major-General J. E. B. Seely, who had told him that 'some soldiers in a YMCA hut' responded to a speaker who urged them to put a stop to the 'odious and capitalist war' by 'retiring when the attack came', so that 'the line was broken through by the enemy in the place they should have filled'. He produced a telegram from Seely saying: 'I have no doubt that seditious propaganda behind our lines prior to [the] German attack [in] March 1918 was [the] direct cause of [the] loss of [the] lives of thousands of brave and loyal British soldiers.' However, the *Liverpool Echo* of the same date quoted the 'Londoner' column of the *Evening Standard* to the effect that General Gough, who commanded the Fifth Army in 1918, Sir Vincent Kell (head of MI5) and Sir Geoffrey Fielding, who commanded the Guards Division, 'have all found themselves unable to support General Seely's statement'. The British Communist Party, in their official comment on the story, published in the *Liverpool Post* of 25 October, observed that

> it is not the least significant point of General Seely's letter that the 'Communist' share in the failure of the BEF to hold back four times their number of German divisions at the junction of their line with the French should have escaped his memory for six-and-a-half years and only come to light in the course of what Mr. Sidney Webb prophesied would be a 'very dirty election'.

The only passage in General Gough's own book *The March Retreat* (1934) which bears any relation to the Chilcott–Seely story refers to an incident early in 1918 when

> it was reported to me that a civilian who was touring the front got on a wagon in the streets of Péronne, and from this extemporised platform addressed all and sundry who were in the streets of the ruined town. He told the soldiers there that 'everyone at home was fed up to the back teeth' – that 'if only the soldiers would refuse to fight there would be peace'! (p. 42)

Gough commented: 'If the soldiers of the Fifth Army had refused to fight (and this gentleman, in company with all his fellow-countrymen may thank God that they did not!), the only peace which we could have obtained would have been one dictated by the Germans after a disastrous and disgraceful retreat.' Actually, those soldiers stood up remarkably well to the onslaught of Von Hutier's army. A. Farrar-Hockley says, in his life of the Fifth Army's commander (*Goughie*, 1975, p. 290): 'It is extraordinary to discover that the number of men who had taken advantage of the confusion to absent themselves from the firing line was negligible – less than one-half per cent . . . The weight of evidence suggests that, with few exceptions, those who scattered rallied to any officer in the vicinity and returned at once to the fighting line.' Here it seems appropriate to recall what Trotsky had written in 1915, in one of his war-correspondent reports to *Kievskaya Mysl*: 'French soldiers express most flattering views about the British Army. Every British soldier is individually his own officer. These men are independent, courageous, resourceful, and unbeatable in defence' (*Yevropa v Voine* [1927], p. 26).

The momentary setback suffered by the Fifth Army needs no such arcane explanation as that offered by the Chilcott–Seely story. The Fifth 'had the longest frontage of any of Haig's four other [*sic*] armies, 42 miles, yet had the least number of men to go round' (J. Toland, *No Man's Land* [1980], p. 4). 'Gough and the Fifth Army had resisted enemies three times as numerous, had made a fighting retreat to the last ditch and had there stood and expended their strength until the few survivors were relieved, and it is difficult to say what more they could have done' (C. Carrington, *Soldier from the Wars Returning* [1965], p. 215). General Gough was deprived of his command and kept under a cloud for years after 1918, as scapegoat for what happened on his sector of the front in March. Toland is probably not far wrong in suggesting that the Liberal politicians in power in London were glad to take revenge on him for his part in the so-called 'officers' mutiny' (against the coercion of Ulster) at the Curragh in 1914 (Toland, 1980, p. 9). It may or may not be significant that Seely had been Secretary of State for War during that affair. Incidentally, by the time Seely (having become Lord Mottistone) wrote the volume of his autobiography covering this period (*Adventure* [1930]) he seems to have forgotten all about the sensational story of events in 1918 which brought him into the headlines in 1924.[25]

6 Sovdepia under German Pressure

Between March and May of 1918, a period when the war in France was going badly for the Allies and well for the Germans (though not as well as had been hoped by their Supreme Command), the Germans extended their power over large parts of European Russia.[1] Thanks to their separate peace treaty with the anti-Bolshevik regime in Kiev they were able to occupy the whole of the Ukraine – and then proceeded, in flagrant contempt of their treaty with Soviet Russia, to push on beyond even the borders claimed by the extremest Ukrainian nationalist, into the Crimea and part of the Don territory.[2] The new Muscovy was to be cut off, as of old, from all independent access to the sea: after the Baltic coast, that of the Black Sea must be brought under German control. Not only, moreover, would the German occupation of the Ukraine oblige Soviet Russia to depend in her foreign relations on the courtesy of Germany – it would deprive her of her principal source of grain. This grain was desperately needed by Germany (and Austria-Hungary), in order to break the British blockade on food imports.[3] To the north, German military aid to the 'Whites' in the civil war in Finland would enable Germany, it was hoped, to gain control of Soviet Russia's last remaining possible 'window to the West', her Murman coastline: where, furthermore, as already mentioned, a U-boat base might be established which would be of great value in the naval conflict with Britain.

The successful operations of the German armed forces to the north of them, in Finland, and to the south, in the Ukraine, meant that in this period 'the position of the Soviet Government was severely shaken, its continued existence seriously threatened'. This assessment by Ludendorff was corroborated by Chicherin, who wrote that the treaty of Brest-Litovsk 'enabled Germany during the succeeding half-year constantly to threaten the Soviet order itself, the very existence of the Soviet republic'.[4] A Damocles' sword hung over the Bolshevik regime. The best-informed and clearest-minded of its leaders realised that their only hope of survival lay in Germany's defeat – although, of course, they could not say so. Captain Sadoul, who was close to them, wrote on 29 March of their fear that a German victory in the war would make the Brest-Litovsk settlement 'definitive' and lead to 'the fall of the revolutionary government'.[5]

An important section of the rulers of Germany remained unsatisfied with Brest-Litovsk and favoured a march on Petrograd and Moscow in the spring of 1918, the ousting of the Bolsheviks and installation of a reactionary puppet government such as the Germans helped to establish, under 'Hetman' Skoropadskii, in the Ukraine. Princess Blücher wrote of the talk in her circles in Berlin immediately after the signing of the peace treaty: 'The Germans here are all boasting of the future happy state of the country [Russia] when it has come to know the blessings of Prussian law and order . . . .'[6] Lenin insisted on 5 May that 'the people must be told the bitter truth, simply, calmly and in a straightforward manner: it is possible, and even probable, that the war party will again get the upper hand in Germany (that is, an offensive against us will commence at once) . . .'.[7] On 14 May he repeated the warning: 'Any day, any moment, we must be prepared for and expect changes in [German] politics in the interests of the extremist war party.'[8] The Red troops forming the 'screens', who faced the Germans across the demarcation line, were exhorted by the Bolsheviks' Supreme War Council to show both extreme vigilance and firm restraint, 'in view of the fact that there is in Germany an extreme party which is not satisfied even with the predatory Brest peace, and which is apparently in the ascendancy . . .'.[9] When harvest-time came, might not the Germans advance 'into the depths of Russia, in order to seize her grain?'[10] And would they stop before they got to Moscow? And what then? Albert Rhys Williams, an active sympathiser with the Bolsheviks who was on the spot in those days, recalled, referring to the last week in April 1918: 'Now, most of the Bolsheviks I spoke to harboured the suspicion that their tenure of power would be brief' (*Journey Into Revolution* [1969], p. 275).

The German documents show that this was no paranoid fantasy on the part of the Bolsheviks. General Groener, chief of staff at the German headquarters in the Ukraine, wrote to his wife on 6 May of the possibility that the German troops in Finland might march on Petrograd, while 'we from the South' march on Moscow.[11] On 16 May a meeting of top German industrialists sent a letter to the Kaiser's Economics Minister, calling for the occupation of the entire northern coast of Russia, so as to bring that country into complete commercial dependence on Germany.[12] About this same time a member of the German commission for the repatriation of prisoners-of-war gave an interview in which he spoke openly of circumstances in which the Germans would be obliged to occupy Petrograd.[13] On 24 May Major Henning, representing the Berlin War Ministry in Moscow, put up a proposal that five divisions be brought back from the West and used to crush the Bolsheviks.[14] But that was easier said than done. General Hoffmann mentioned the difficulty in his diary entry for 25 May: 'I should have no objection to pushing farther and farther eastwards – I should like to get to India, except that the distances grow more immense, and our army does not'[15] – a reference to the heavy losses being suffered in the West.

The insuperable argument against unlimited eastward adventures was that more and more troops were needed on the Western Front. Though the offensive in France was making progress, it was not going according to schedule, and losses were unexpectedly heavy. Transfers of troops from east to west had, therefore, to continue through April and May. It was for this reason that the small Allied Force at Murmansk was considerably enlarged and made more enterprising. Balfour wrote to the British Ambassador in Washington on 19 April that the Germans were still moving divisions westward, and might bring over another fifteen. This process had to be stopped – 'and nothing will do this save German anxiety in the East'.[16] On 29 July Churchill was able to report to Parliament in these terms:

> Up to the time we landed in Murmansk in May 1918, German divisions were passing from the Eastern to the Western Front at an average rate of six divisions per month to attack the Allied forces. From the time we had landed there not another division was sent from the Eastern Front. . . .[17]

Paradoxically, this development had the effect of improving the Soviet Government's position in relation to the Germans, by weakening the case for the 'forward policy' advocated by Ludendorff, Hoffmann and their co-thinkers. So long as it was known in Russia that the Allies were holding their own against the German offensive and even compelling the Germans to take special steps to cope with their counter-measures, anti-Bolshevik political groups within the country were encouraged not to yield to a 'pro-German orientation' – not to compete, that is, with the Bolsheviks in appeasing Germany and, in particular, not to offer to accept the treaty of Brest-Litovsk. In this situation, so long as the Bolsheviks showed themselves willing to co-operate in essentials with the Germans, the most economical policy for the latter would be to leave them in power and even provide them with some positive support. However regrettable some of his activities might be, Lenin was the only 'viceroy' available to the Kaiser in Central Russia.

A Western observer, writing on 17 April 1918, noted the subservience of the Soviet Government to German bullying. 'The People's Commissars groan and bow their heads. The only hope left to them lies in the victory of that France, called bourgeois and imperialist, which they have so badly betrayed but which will perhaps compel Germany to slacken its grip.'[18] The German Ambassador was able to report on 29 April that when he talked with Chicherin, the Commissar referred to the German advances in Finland and the Ukraine only in hints and in a melancholy tone.[19] A Frenchman who talked with Chicherin on 1 May was provoked, when the Commissar spoke of Russia's need for a respite from hostilities, to remark that this was 'a respite that you obtain at the cost of French blood. What would become of you if France were not holding the German Army? You would be conquered, subjugated right up to the Urals.' Chicherin replied that if Russia were to resume the war with Germany, 'the Germans would inevitably seize Petrograd and Moscow'. The Frenchman noted the difference between Chicherin's resigned acceptance of German occupation of large areas of his country and his loud denunciation of the Japanese.[20] That difference was clearly explained in the decision of the Bolshevik Party's Central Committee, taken on 6 May, 'to yield to the German ultimatum [concerning Fort Ino, on the border with Finland]. The British ultimatum to be rejected. (For war against Germany threatens greater losses and calamities than against Japan).'[21] The point was reiterated by Lenin on 13 May: 'The danger of the Japanese advance can more easily be paralysed (or can be delayed for a longer time) than the threat of the Germans occupying Petrograd, Moscow and a large part of European Russia.'[22]

The Soviet Government was prepared, in this period, not merely to submit to aggression from Germany but also to make positive gestures of appeasement. On 14 May concessions were offered to Germany for the exploitation of the iron ore of Krivoi Rog and other mineral resources. As Debo comments: 'The Soviet proposals indicated that the Bolsheviks were not only prepared to abide by the treaty of Brest-Litovsk but, if allowed to do so, were even willing to provide Germany with the economic reinforcement it needed in the last phase of the Great War.'[23]

A special difficulty, however, which impeded the Moscow Government in its pursuit of its policy of 'neutrality of a special type' was the militancy of the local Bolsheviks in the Ukraine and neighbouring areas, occupied or directly threatened by the Germans.[24] On 4 April V. P. Zatonskii informed Moscow, from Rostov, that the Bolsheviks in the southern areas were considering the formation of a 'union of southern republics', bringing together the Ukraine with the Don and the Kuban. Stalin sent a sharp reply, forbidding any such move, which, since the Don and the Kuban were claimed as units in the Russian Soviet Federative Socialist Republic (RSFSR), would involve Moscow in the Ukrainian comrades' war with the Germans.[25] On 24 April, so as not to offend the Germans, order was given for any of Antonov-Ovseyenko's 'Ukrainian' Bolshevik troops crossing into the Don region to be disarmed.[26] Talks began at Kursk on 29 April between Soviet Russian representatives and those of the Ukrainian puppet government, to settle frontier disputes and other outstanding problems. Nevertheless, the Germans continued to act as they saw fit in the south-eastern direction. A delegation from the Don Soviet Republic came to Taganrog on 1 May to 'demand' that the Germans refrain from invading their territory, which was to be regarded as an integral part of the Russian Soviet Republic. The German general replied that his orders were to take Rostov-on-Don, as a place of strategic importance, and this he proceeded to do a few days later. The government of the Don Soviet Republic withdrew to Tsaritsyn.[27] And on 2 May Rakovskii, head of Moscow's delegation dealing with Ukrainian matters, informed Antonov-Ovseyenko: 'We must liquidate the affair with the Ukraine, at least temporarily, until a more favourable historical situation arrives . . . We must ensure that the German army, pursuing our troops, advances no further.'[28]

The compliant and helpful attitude of the Bolshevik Government in Moscow convinced the Germans that there was no need to take urgent military measures against it. That was good news for them, in that all possible forces were needed to 'finish the job' in the West. German policy was dominated, for the time being at least, by that section of the ruling class which considered (in the words of a Soviet historian) that, 'with a view to waging the war successfully in the West, Germany should not fight against Soviet Russia, so as to avoid a war on two fronts'.[29] By the middle of May this tendency was effectively predominant, and advances into Central Russia by German troops came to a halt. When Admiral von Müller, on 19 May, said to the Kaiser that 'this was very gratifying. In our present situation there were more important things to think of than a little more booty,' the All-Highest replied: 'Yes, we were doing our best to drive the Russians into the arms of the Entente.'[30] A memorandum by Foreign Minister Kühlmann, dated 22 May, stressed that Germany must uphold the Soviet Government in order to keep Russia weak. A *united* Russia would inevitably side with the Allies.[31] The position is well summarised by the Soviet historian Kholodkovskii: 'A Soviet Government in Russia, observing the Brest peace treaty, was from the German standpoint preferable to a government which, though bourgeois, would be hostile to Germany.' As Kholodkovskii goes on to note, however, 'what would be incomparably more to Germany's advantage would be to have in Russia a pro-German bourgeois government . . . Even after the Brest peace Germany was preparing for the near future, as soon as convenient, to go to war against the country with which she had just made peace.'[32]

The necessary pre-condition for an anti-Bolshevik 'crusade' by the Germans was victory in the West. Once the Allies had been crushed, Germany ought certainly to be able to find in Russia some suitable 'Muscovite Skoropadskii' to replace Lenin, for, after a victory for Germany in the West, only crazy idealists would stick to their 'pro-Entente orientation': all serious political elements would be obliged to adapt themselves to a world wherein Germany held unchallenged control of Russia's fate.

Once it had become clear to him that Germany was, for reasons of her own and for the time being, ready to tolerate the survival of his regime within certain restricted frontiers, Lenin resolved to adapt his policy accordingly and enter into a quasi-alliance with Germany. 'In May', writes Debo, 'when Lenin was certain that, for the moment, the Germans could not afford to smash his regime, he turned decisively against any policy of co-operation with the Allies. Lockhart was left to gnash his teeth in bitter disappointment.'[33] The implications of this 'qualitative change' in Soviet policy, let it be recalled, were felt with particular keenness by the Red Finns. As mentioned earlier, when their leader Tokoi asked whether Lenin had any objection to their joining in an organised way with the British at Murmansk, he had replied that 'under the terms of the Brest-Litovsk treaty Russia could not answer that question outright, let alone officially approve such a step. But, in a way he had, he winked his left eye slightly and said: "If the English want to help you, then let them help you." '[34] Now, however, Tokoi and his men found themselves repudiated as traitors. Finland, Karelia and the Kola Peninsula were to be abandoned to the White Finns and their German backers. Chicherin informed the Murman District Soviet on 22 May that 'in view of the general political situation it is quite inadmissible to turn to the British for aid . . . It may be that the British themselves will fight against the invading White Guards, but we must not act as their allies, and we shall protest against their operations on our territory.'[35]

Before leaving Finland and North Russia, it is appropriate to add to what has already been said about the importance of this region to the Allies. Kennan quotes a report written by an American official, Arthur Bullard, in early May 1918, when he travelled from Moscow to Archangel, in which he describes the impression made upon him by the stocks of supplies sent by Russia's Allies which the Soviet Government's 'Extraordinary Evacuation Commission' was busily shifting southward to who-knew-what destination. There was barbed wire, small arms, ammunition, shells, artillery, trucks, field kitchens, ambulances, railway carriage wheels, axles, rails, coils of copper telegraph wire and much else.

> It was worth its weight in gold to Berlin. It was all so terribly needed by our friends before Amiens, on the Chemin des Dames. So much of it would be valuable to our own men when the time would come . . . The wasted efforts of all the staunch citizens behind the lines in the factories of France and England and America to hurry the production of this material! The cool heroism of the sailor folks who had brought it through minefields and submarines![36]

Submarines were, indeed, very much in the minds of those responsible for directing Allied activity on the shores of the Barents Sea. Besides safeguarding such stores as were left in Russia's northern ports, and besides discouraging German troop-transfers to the west, this activity was motivated by fear, as already mentioned, of the establishment of a German submarine base somewhere along the Kola Peninsula. Early in May, as we have seen, a German-backed expedition by the Finnish Whites approached Pechenga (Petsamo) and was beaten off by British marines and Finnish Reds.[37] On the same day (12 May), E. H. Carr wrote a minute saying: 'We clearly cannot withdraw from Murmansk and leave the coast clear for the Germans, whether the Bolsheviks ask us to or not.'[38] Field Marshal Ironside commented on the seriousness of the threat: 'Could they but establish a submarine base there, the whole of our complicated defences . . . would be turned, with dire results to our convoy system.'[39] And General Maynard assessed the situation thus:

> Had she [Germany] succeeded in this [submarine-base project], it is certain she would have taken an increased toll of our Atlantic shipping, which at that time included scores of transports conveying American troops to Europe. For the ocean route from Murmansk to the Atlantic was free of minefields, and the area to be patrolled by our anti-submarine craft would have been extended so enormously as to banish all hope of efficient counter-measures to cope with the new danger.[40]

It was therefore not a matter for surprise to anyone that the Allies decided to step up their intervention in North Russia when they learnt, in the last days of May, that Soviet Russia had decided, under German pressure, to cede the western part of the Murman Coast, with Pechenga, to Germany's client state, White Finland.[41]

During May, before the final turn towards quasi-alliance with Germany was completed, the opponents of that policy within the Bolshevik leadership made a last effort to prevent it. The British public learnt of this through the despatches sent to the *Manchester Guardian* by its correspondent in Russia, Morgan Philips Price. In the issue of 7 May appeared a message he had sent on 3 May, reporting the view held in some circles in Moscow that

> the close proximity of the Central Powers makes the latter the most dangerous enemy . . . England and America, being farther away, are felt to be less dangerous to the Soviet Republic . . . I hear from well-informed sources that the idea of mutual co-operation between England, America and Russia with a view to resisting the Central Empires has support in certain Soviet quarters.

The issue of 31 May carried a message dated 15 May in which he said that there was a tendency, headed by Sokolnikov, which held that the Germans, after restoring the old order in the Ukraine, would soon proceed to try and do the same in Great Russia ('the military party has definitely won'), and that therefore the policy of neutrality should give way to 'closer contact with the Allies'. Although this view was held by 'an influential minority', Party discipline inhibited its public expression. As we know now, the Bolshevik Party's Central Committee had, in fact, at its meeting on 10–13 May, rejected a resolution moved by Sokolnikov along the lines indicated by Price. The change of regime in the Ukraine (the replacement of the Rada by Skoropadskii), it was urged, signified that the Russian bourgeoisie had now lined up with German imperialism, and a German onslaught in the near future was inevitable. The 'breathing-space' was at an end, and all-out war must be prepared for. 'At the same time, it is necessary to conclude a military agreement with the Anglo-French coalition, with a view to military co-operation on certain conditions.' The contrary standpoint, advanced by Lenin, was approved, everyone present voting with him, except for Sokolnikov and Stalin.[42] When the Bolsheviks were forced to give up their attempt to ride two horses at once, 'under pressure from Berlin, they chose a stallion sired in Germany. They were freed from their perilous ride only by the defeat of Germany at the hands of the Allies.'[43]

7 The Czechoslovak Revolt and its Consequences

As if the constant threat from Germany were not enough, the Bolsheviks, in this same crucial month of May, brought upon themselves a fresh danger, in the form of the revolt of the Czechoslovak Legion. It would, perhaps, be unfair to see this 'own goal', this self-inflicted wound, as the result of mere ineptitude. It was the contradictions of their situation that compelled the Bolsheviks to take the steps that led to so disastrous an outcome.

The Czechoslovak Legion co-operated with the Bolshevik (and Left SR) forces resisting the German advance into the Ukraine in February and March, playing a particularly important role in the battle of Bakhmach. General Hoffmann wrote of this period that 'we had many fierce engagements with the Czechoslovak divisions'.[1] The Bolshevik commander in the Ukraine, Antonov-Ovseyenko, formally thanked them in an army order: 'The revolutionary armies of South Russia will never forget the brotherly aid which was granted by the Czech Corps in the struggle of the labouring people against the hordes of base imperialism.'[2]

After the peace of Brest-Litovsk, since they could no longer expect to fight for their cause on Russian territory with the consent of the Soviet Government, the Czechoslovaks negotiated with Moscow for facilities to leave the country and go to France, to fight on the Western Front. At first it seemed that there would be no problem. Antonov-Ovseyenko records that on 19 March, at a meeting of the Soviet Government's Supreme War Council in Moscow, Trotsky said that it should be possible to evacuate the Czechoslovaks through one Russian port or another. Nothing was said about disarming them. Antonov-Ovseyenko was therefore surprised when, soon afterward, he received a telegram from the Penza Province Soviet urging care in dealings with the Czechoslovaks and deploring attempts to take away their weapons. What was going on? He forwarded the telegram to Trotsky, adding a note of his own: 'Be careful with the Czechs, we shall need them.'[3] *He* doubtless had in mind a possible resumption of the war with Germany. But Trotsky's was a different scenario, based on a different 'need'.

The Soviet Government desperately needed trained and politically reliable troops to keep it in power. As a nucleus for the Red Army in process of formation, it had Lettish units of the old army and a substantial body of Hungarian ex-prisoners of war – troops who were conveniently separated by nationality and language from the population they were required to overawe. The Czechoslovaks would be a valuable addition to these janissaries. On 20 March Trotsky urged Sadoul and Riggs, the American assistant military attaché, to let the Czechoslovaks stay in Russia and join the Red Army. On the same day, an order went out for trains carrying the Czechoslovak soldiers to be stopped.[4]

On 27 March Trotsky announced the launching of an agitational campaign among the Czechoslovak troops, with a view to winning them for the Red Army. According to the Czech Colonel Hurban, in a report to President Masaryk, 'this agitation was carried on vigorously and not by very honest methods'.[5] On 3 April Strombach, the Czech Communist who was directing this agitation at Penza, informed Moscow that he had asked the local Soviet to give him the fullest facilities for his work. We have seen that the Penza Soviet was originally dubious as to the wisdom of the policy being followed, but as soon as Strombach had succeeded in making some recruits, they were won over – 'convinced' that by the obstruction of their evacuation 'the Legion would be unnerved and ultimately become so disgusted with its journey to France that it would revolt against its "reactionary" political and military leadership and join the Soviets'. The Czechoslovak Communists issued a leaflet for distribution among the Legionaries which said: 'A real socialist will not quit Russia, for free Russia needs real fighters for freedom.'[6]

The Czechoslovaks, already irritated by this treatment, were alarmed when they intercepted a secret cable from Chicherin to the Krasnoyarsk Soviet, dated 21 April, which read: 'Fearing that Japan will advance into Siberia, Germany is categorically demanding that German prisoners of war held in Eastern Siberia be removed at once to either Western Siberia or European Russia. Use all possible means. The Czechoslovaks must not go further East.'[7] The movement westward of the repatriated German, Austrian and Hungarian war prisoners subjected the patience of the Czechoslovaks to further stress, especially when the trains carrying them passed through the stations where the Czechoslovaks were perforce marking time. A historian of the Legion epitomised thus the bitter feelings of those men: 'Here are we, struggling to reach France to help the Allies, and yet not only are we unable to move forward, but we actually have to permit fresh and thoroughly rested enemy soldiers to slip through our hands back to the Fatherland, so that they may be ready to fight us when eventually we reach the Western Front.'[8]

An 'incident' was bound to occur sooner or later, and on 14 May it did. A trainload of Hungarians arrived at Chelyabinsk, where some Czechoslovaks were in a siding. As the Hungarians' train moved on its way westward, a lump of iron was thrown from it at a group of Czechoslovak soldiers on the platform, and one of them, František Duchácek, was knocked unconscious and fell on the track, where he was nearly run over by the next train. His comrades pursued the Hungarian train, brought it to a halt, and demanded that the man who threw the iron be identified and handed over to the appropriate authorities. Ensign Hruška impressed on the Hungarians that the situation was extremely dangerous and they had better do what he said. This was put to them in Hungarian, Romanian and German. The only result was provocative and scornful gestures, whereupon Hruška threatened to shoot every tenth man if they did not obey. This produced cries of abuse, and one of the Hungarians shouted at the Czechoslovaks something extremely offensive. Many of the Czechoslovaks were Slovaks who had served in Hungarian regiments and knew the language. It was more than they could take, and a violent scrimmage ensued.[9]

The local Bolshevik authorities intervened and in the course of their investigation, a number of Czechoslovaks whom they had summoned as witnesses were arrested and imprisoned. A delegation sent by the Czechoslovaks to demand these men's release were also placed under arrest. On 17 May the Czechoslovaks released the prisoners by force. 'The Chelyabinsk affair' was soon settled peacefully by the local disputants: but it had provided Moscow with the pretext to deal firmly with all those Czechoslovaks who declined to join the Red Army of their own free will. On 20 May Trotsky's assistant, Aralov, telegraphed an order to the soviets all along the railway between Penza and Omsk. They were to de-train the Czechoslovaks and either organise them into 'labour artels' or draft them, willy-nilly, into the Red Army. This telegram was intercepted by the Czechoslovaks.[10] On 25 May Trotsky himself despatched a telegram to the same addressees. All Czechoslovaks were to be disarmed. Any Czechoslovak found armed was to be shot on the spot. Every group in which even one armed man was found was to be rounded up and put in a prisoner-of-war-camp.[11]

When the Soviet authorities tried to enforce this order, they met with determined resistance. The forces at their disposal were very limited, and in some cases they employed German and Austro-Hungarian war prisoners who, rather than return home, had enlisted in the Red Army, to attempt the disarmament of the Czechoslovaks, which naturally enraged the latter even more, and convinced many of them that they were victims of a plot engineered by the Central Powers.[12] A Soviet historian has characterised Trotsky's order as 'criminal adventurism', given the lack of adequate Red forces in the Urals and Siberia to put it into effect.[13] But Radek, discussing the affair with Lockhart on 6 June, told him that 'they could not consent to leave the Czechs their arms without risk of serious complications with the counter-revolutionaries and with the Germans, who would be more than ever convinced of a secret understanding between the Allies and the Bolsheviks.'[14]

Whatever excuse may be given for Trotsky's action, its consequences were far-reaching. When recognising his subsequent achievement in defeating the Czechoslovaks in battle, the historian ought not to forget that, in a sense, it was he who had raised up that enemy in the first place. Peter Fleming wrote, most pertinently, that Trotsky's

> off-with-their-heads order of 25 May reveals very clearly two things. First, [his] belief that he had the scattered Czech echelons at his mercy; second, his fear that the Legion was or might become a danger to the state . . . Trotsky's belief was a fallacy; his fear, if not far-fetched, was of a remote contingency. The action he took, or tried to take, against the Czechs was deluded. It was meant to liquidate a minor, potential threat to Soviet interests. What it did was to call into being a threat to which neither of these epithets could be applied.[15]

Until now the armed counter-revolution in European Russia had meant only Krasnov's Don Cossacks and Dutov's Orenburg Cossacks, neither of them keen to leave their home territories, and the Volunteer Army, confined by Krasnov and the Germans to Northern Caucasia. The Czechoslovaks, however, encouraged by the Allies, linked up with the numerous anti-Bolshevik elements between the Urals and the Volga, and launched an offensive aimed at capturing Moscow, ousting the Soviet Government (seen as Germany's puppet) and restoring the Eastern Front against Germany. A period of acute danger opened for the Bolsheviks. Looking back in 1920, Preobrazhenskii wrote of the summer of 1918 that 'it was the only time when the Soviet Government might have fallen under the blows of its numerous enemies'.[16]

During the weeks between the Czechoslovak revolt at the end of May and the murder of Count Mirbach early in July there were not a few signs that the tendency in German ruling circles which favoured a march on Petrograd and Moscow might, after all, gain ascendancy. Mirbach wrote to the Reich Chancellor at the beginning of June about signs of impending collapse of Soviet power and the need to take measures in view of a possible 'regrouping' of forces in Russia – to which Hertling replied: 'Agreed; but *very* cautiously.'[17] Ludendorff expressed his view on 9 June: 'We can expect nothing from this Soviet Government' and urged 'vigorous and ruthless' action against it.[18] General Groener wrote to his wife on 14 June about the weakness of the Bolsheviks' position and complained that only German support kept them in power.[19] On 25 June Mirbach warned his Minister of the possibility that the pro-Allied Right SRs, backed by the Czechoslovaks, might come to power in Moscow, and urged action to forestall them by establishing 'a regime that corresponds to *our* wishes and interests'.[20] An intelligence report received by the British Foreign Office on 29 June from the naval attaché in Petrograd, allegedly based on information from Ludendorff's headquarters, stated that the German General Staff considered that within a month their attack on the Western Front would render the Allied armies incapable of taking the offensive for a long time: the Germans would then turn upon Russia, tear up the peace treaty, and proclaim a monarchy.[21] Some confirmation of this forecast is provided by an entry in Groener's diary for 29 June: 'Ludendorff seems to want to march soon against the Bolsheviks. Two days ago came a query from *Oberost* as to whether we could take Kursk and Bryansk with our forces.'[22]

The Soviet Government's response to this threatening situation was to redouble its efforts at appeasement of Germany. When, on 10 June, the Kuban Bolsheviks launched an attack across the Sea of Azov against German-occupied Taganrog, Lenin rebuked them and gave strict orders that the demarcation line be respected,[23] and on 12 June the Bolsheviks throughout Northern Caucasia were ordered from Tsaritsyn to cease operations against the Germans (who had occupied Bataisk and the tip of the Taman Peninsula) and to start negotiations with them so as to prevent any more clashes.[24] The scuttling of the Black Sea Fleet at Novorossiisk was aimed at preventing either of two possible developments: if the Germans were allowed to take over the ships they might use them to attack Novorossiisk, and if the Left-SR sailors who wanted to use the ships to attack the Germans in the Crimea got their way, that would certainly provoke serious reprisals. Raskolnikov warned the sailors that the Germans were 'at Narva and Pskov', and would seize Petrograd if hostilities should be renewed.[25] Krassin wrote to his wife from Berlin on 16 June:

> There is no doubt that some of the Bolshevik troops do not keep to their lines, and then when the Germans retaliate by attacking them, they become almost hysterical in their indignation . . . We certainly cannot fight at present, we have to develop a stronger national physique before it will be possible to show any power of resistance.[26]

Anti-British gestures were now multiplied by the Soviet Government. Lockhart reported that Uritsky had told the Petrograd Soviet on 22 June that the British were behind the murder of Volodarskii.[27] That same day, the British Consul at Archangel reported that the Soviet authorities had demanded the removal from the port of all the British ships there which were engaged in evacuating whatever was left in the Allies' supply-dumps. (E. H. Carr minuted on that report: 'The answer to this seems to be that as the material and explosives in question are Allied property and the local authorities or the central government have obstructed every attempt by the Allies to remove them, it is necessary to keep a warship there to guard them. Meanwhile, as there is evidently the chance of a quarrel, our forces at Archangel ought to be strengthened as much as possible.') Lockhart informed the Foreign Office on 26 June that Trotsky had told an officer of the French military mission that the Small Sovnarkom had accepted in principle that the only way to avert German intervention and the consequent occupation of Moscow and Petrograd was for the Bolsheviks to take a strong line against the Allies everywhere.[28]

What forces did the Soviet Government possess with which it could carry out such a policy? The Red Army was deployed chiefly along the demarcation line with the German-occupied territories, forming the so-called 'screens'. Given the threatening attitude sometimes adopted by the German military, and their occasional encroachments, would it be safe to withdraw large numbers of men from the 'screens'? According to a statement made by Chicherin on 24 June, this had to be done. The People's Commissar for Foreign Affairs insisted most strongly that sending forces to Murmansk was incomparably more important than keeping substantial forces in Pskov and Vitebsk provinces, facing the Germans. Natsarenus, in charge of operations to evict the Allies from Murmansk, must without delay be given the forces he needed to do that job.[29] A proposal made to the Germans at this time is recorded by Major von Bothmer, of the prisoners-of-war repatriation commission, in his diary entry of 23 June. The Germans should allow all those of their POWs who were still in Siberia and the region between the Volga and the Urals to be armed by the Soviet authorities so that they could take part, alongside the Red Army, in fighting the Czechoslovaks. As soon as these men had successfully accomplished their task, the Soviets would expedite their return home (and so to the Western Front).[30] The proposal was rejected: but, all the same, the Germans now showed themselves much readier to co-operate with the Bolsheviks.

Prince Rupprecht had appreciated at the beginning of June that Germany could no longer expect to win the war by victory on the Western Front. A couple of weeks later the German Foreign Minister, Kühlmann, came round to the same view, and in a speech in the Reichstag on 24 June admitted that it was unlikely that the war could be ended by purely military means. So public and forthright an admission was scandalous, and Kühlmann was removed from office, to be replaced by Admiral Hintze. But Hintze found himself a prisoner of the same hard facts as his predecessor, and could not concur with the militarists and others who hoped that, unlike Kühlmann, he would support them in their desire to take over Soviet Russia by armed force forthwith. There were simply not the troops available, in view of the persistent refusal of the Allies in France to give way. The Supreme Command had to say so when even such a modest proposal as the occupation of Novorossiisk was put forward.[31] Already on 9 June the press review sent home by Wardrop, the British Consul in Moscow, had included news from Riga that all fit men, including Landsturm soldiers who had been re-examined, were being transferred to France. Their morale was low: they 'no longer believe victory probable'.[32] General Groener wrote to his wife on 30 June that it was becoming ever clearer that the outcome of the battle under way in the West would be decisive also for the solution of Germany's problems in the East.[33]

A political development resulting from the Czechoslovak revolt had an important bearing on German policy in Russia. Many of the anti-Bolshevik elements inside Soviet Russia who had been fighting along with the Germans now saw the Allied-backed forces advancing on Moscow from the East as their chief hope, and so gave up their 'pro-German orientation'. Numerous officers made their way clandestinely to join Kappel and the other Russian military men who were co-operating with the Czechoslovaks. These events strengthened the argument of those in the German Foreign Office who insisted that, distasteful as it might be, there was no alternative to the Soviet Government as a reliable ally.[34] As a corollary, the Germans' conduct in relation to the Volunteer Army hardened. Whereas, earlier, they had allowed officers to make their way through the Ukraine to join Denikin, and even tolerated recruiting centres for his army in places under their occupation, they now put a stop to all that. With a view to weakening the Volunteer Army, they promoted the formation of breakaway groups – the 'Southern Army' and the 'Astrakhan Army' – led by men who were either adventurers or else monarchists unhappy with Denikin's non-committal attitude on the constitutional question. These groups did little or no fighting against the Bolsheviks, but served to introduce confusion into the anti-Bolshevik camp.[35]

What specially concerned the Germans in connection with the Volunteer Army was the possibility of a link-up between Denikin and the Czechoslovaks. Krasnov, after all, might not be completely reliable, or might fall. On 30 June Chicherin reassured Mirbach that there was no danger of the Czechoslovaks getting through to Rostov, because Tsaritsyn was firmly held by Soviet troops. Chicherin had just spoken to Stalin, who was in charge there, and could promise the German Ambassador that he had nothing to worry about.[36] In principle, of course, it would have been the ideal solution for the Germans simply to march into Northern Caucasia, from Bataisk and Taman, and 'liquidate' the Volunteer Army. Such an operation, if successful, would, besides eliminating an enemy force, have given them access to the Grozny oilfield. But where were the men to do it? (Answer: fighting the French and British in France.) General Knörzer's small force of three infantry divisions and one cavalry brigade was responsible for the whole 'quadrilateral' Taganrog–Rostov–Millerovo–Bakhmut, and could not spare sufficient troops to dispose of the Volunteers. Besides, as Denikin noted: 'An advance by the German forces into Northern Caucasia would, given the high mobility of the Volunteer Army, entail the risk of a long-drawn-out operation, with all the invaders' communications exposed to attacks by partisan units.'[37]

Confidence on the part of the Soviet Government that, for the time being, at least, the Germans had abandoned aggressive intentions towards them was strengthened by the agreement of the German Supreme Army Command, on 26 June, to form mixed commissions for settling the 'incidents' that occurred from time to time along the demarcation line.[38] And still more, perhaps, by the Germans' failure to react in face of the nationalisation decree of 28 June, despite its effect on German property.[39] That the Soviet Government was well aware of what lay behind the passivity of the Germans at this time is shown by the reply returned on 1 July by the War Commissariat to an objection concerning the transfer of Red troops from the 'screens' to the front against the Czechoslovaks ('would not the Germans take advantage?') by pointing out that any dangerous move by the Germans was now most unlikely, first and foremost because they were too much tied up on the Western Front.[40]

On 2 July a conference was held at Spa, the German Army's headquarters on the Western Front, between the Reich Government and the Supreme Command, at which the Russian question was discussed. A telegram had just been received from the Foreign Office in Berlin stating that Joffe, the Soviet ambassador, 'gives us a firm guarantee of oil from Baku'. This was highly important: as Admiral von Capelle, representing the Admiralty, observed, 'the U-boat campaign is dependent on oil'.[41] It was decided that '*for the present* [emphasis in the original]' the fall of the Bolsheviks should not be induced, but the Germans should keep in close touch with the monarchists in view of future possibilities. Money should go on being provided for Krasnov, but very discreetly: more with a view to discouraging him from joining with the Czechoslovaks than for anti-Soviet activity.[42] The Kaiser continued to cherish hopes that, one day, his unwholesome collaborators in Moscow could be replaced by others more to his taste: 'elements of order', assembled under Germany's wing at Kiev, would set out from there to initiate 'Russia's rebirth'. How he pictured the reborn Russia he revealed in a talk with a representative of Krasnov: it should be divided into five puppet states – Central Russia, Ukraine, the South-East (Don, Kuban, Terek, and so on), Transcaucasia and Siberia.[43]

8 The Mirbach Crisis

Before coming to the crisis in Soviet–German relations provoked by the murder of Count Mirbach and the Left SR revolt, let us take a look at a characteristic Soviet document of this period, namely, a broadsheet in English, 'signed' by Lenin and Chicherin and entitled *Why Have You Come to Murmansk?*[1] It is not dated, but from internal evidence would appear to have been produced in July.[2] The broadsheet begins:

> Comrade! Why have you come to Murmansk? You have been told in England that the demand for men on the Western Front is greater than ever. You know that in England men of 45 and over are being called to the colours because of the urgent need of men in France. Yet you are brought here, right in the Arctic Sea, a thousand miles from the battlefront.

The Murman Railway was 'in no danger from the Germans or the Finns' (nothing was said about the Murman coast.) 'If the Germans want to attack the Murman Railway they must first take Petrograd . . . We are no longer at war with Germany. The Germans cannot advance on Petrograd without first declaring war on us again.' The British soldiers for whom the broadsheet was intended should have no sympathy for the Czechoslovaks. They

> are gathering around themselves the corrupt and reactionary officials of the Tsarist regime. It is the same crowd that betrayed Kitchener, that sold the guns and munitions made in British factories to the Germans, that disorganised our army, and who were just about to sell Russia to the Germans when we made our revolution.

Mentioned in the text of this broadsheet is an incident which occurred at Kem, a station of the Murman Railway, on 2 July – the killing of some members of the local soviet by the Allied forces. This incident often cropped up subsequently in Soviet anti-British propaganda. General Maynard's account of what actually happened runs as follows:

> I ordered disarming of the Red Guards at Kem on 2 July and a search for arms. During the search, a house was entered in which

> the local Soviet was sitting. The members leapt to their feet, two of them drew out their revolvers, and one fired on the Serbians who were carrying out the search. Another threw a bomb, which did not explode. During the struggle which ensued, three members [of the Kem Soviet] were shot.[3]

It is curious that a Soviet account of the struggle of those days and in those parts which was published in 1978, although it mentions events at Kem on 2 July, says absolutely nothing about this affair. On the contrary, a rather friendly picture is drawn of the behaviour of the 'interventionists' on this occasion. When the British occupied the town, we are told, they at first disarmed the Red guerrillas based there, led by G. I. Lezhev. Later, however, they returned the weapons, supplied ammunition and equipment, and authorised Lezhev to undertake operations against the White Finns, which he proceeded to do.[4]

Four days after the Spa conference on 2 July Count Mirbach, the German Ambassador in Moscow, was murdered by Left SRs, who thereupon launched their uprising aimed at renewing the war between Russia and Germany – as a 'revolutionary war', of course. This was the supreme 'moment of truth' in relations between Soviet Russia and Germany in 1918. Far from marching on Petrograd and Moscow, as might have been expected, the Germans confined themselves to demanding that they be allowed to send a small body of troops to the Russian capital to guard their embassy against possible further outrages. And when Lenin refused to agree to that demand, the Germans did not insist. There was great anxiety in some leading Bolshevik circles at this time, regarding the possible German reaction. Paquet, the German Embassy's press secretary, mentions Radek's state of agitation. Would 'the military party in Germany' resume hostilities against Russia? The Bolsheviks were ready to give them 'every satisfaction'.[5] Joffe told Lenin, over the direct wire from Berlin, that 'any blunder, even a petty provocation on our part, will immediately be exploited from the military standpoint'.[6] But Lenin and Chicherin knew better. It appears that Lenin had had a talk with the well-informed Hanecki-Fürstenberg, just back from Berlin.[7] From him he may have learnt that the situation on the Western Front was now not going too well for the

Germans. In any case, when Lockhart spoke to Chicherin about the Soviets' refusal to submit to the Germans' demand to send an embassy guard, he was able to report to the Foreign Office, on 15 July, that the Sovnarkom 'did not think it would lead to any grave measures on the part of the Germans, as they were convinced that the latter were not in a position to embark on any fresh military adventure in Russia'.[8] At the Fifth Congress of Soviets, when Spiridonova, about to start her party's armed action, denounced the Bolsheviks as obedient servants of Mirbach and proclaimed the Left SRs' refusal to recognise the treaty of Brest-Litovsk, 'a French representative rose from his seat in the diplomatic box and solemnly bowed his gratitude for the hullaballoo that he must have mistaken for a tribute to France. There was a moment's silent gasp of astonishment throughout the [Bolshoi] theatre.'[9] The delegates should not have been so astonished: it was indeed the efforts of the Allied armies in France that enabled them to carry on with impunity pursuing their bloody charades. Honest contemporaries had no doubt regarding the factor that saved Soviet Russia at this time. A. F. Ilyin-Zhenevskii, who was working in the Petrograd branch of the War Commissariat, wrote in 1929 of his and his colleagues' state of mind:

> The destiny of our republic again began to hang by a hair. Every day we alternated between despair and hope. Was an evil fate going to drive our exhausted, wounded country once again into war? Were we not to be allowed a breathing-space for peaceful construction? But soon we received reassuring news. At that time Germany was not up to the job of disposing of us. Her whole attention was focused on the Franco-British front, where she was making her last efforts to avoid defeat. And so, when she heard our reply, she put that demand of hers in her pocket, thereby implicitly renouncing it. When we learnt that this had happened we took heart once more.[10]

Doubtless this confidence that the Germans were not likely to go out of their way to make trouble, unless directly provoked, emboldened the Bolsheviks to murder the Imperial family at Ekaterinburg about this time. The failure of the Kaiser to utter any public protest cannot have strengthened such 'pro-German orientation' as remained among the Russian monarchists.

Lenin's friend V. D. Bonch-Bruevich (brother of the General) offers an interesting point of view on the crisis of July 1918:

> The very fact of the revolt by the Left SRs helped us greatly, since it was obvious to all that this gross provocation had come from the ranks of out-and-out enemies of the Soviet power. Such rapid suppression of the new counter-revolutionaries, with capture of the rebels' positions, and the severe way their instigators and ringleaders were dealt with, at once made plain to everyone that our Communist government had a firm grip on power and was not going to show mercy to anyone. Altogether, this undoubtedly made an impression on Germany's ruling circles, and the spectre of almost inevitable war began gradually to fade away. (*Vospominaniya o Lenine*, 2nd edn [1969], p. 320)

Nevertheless, the Soviet Government appreciated that it could not go *too* far in flouting the Germans, who still held some strong cards. Some of the leaders of the Lettish troops who were playing such an important role in maintaining Soviet power secretly approached the German Embassy to ask if Germany would grant them an amnesty so that they could return to their homeland, then under German occupation. What a disaster for the Bolsheviks that would have been! The proposal was rejected for the time being: but Major Schubert, the German military attaché, urged that the possibility of a change of mind be kept dangling before the Letts, as this would help ensure that they opposed the coming to power in Moscow of any government hostile to Germany.[11]

The Germans had to be convinced that the Bolsheviks were sincerely fighting against the Allies, and so, on 7 July, Lenin sent an order to Natsarenus at Petrozavodsk to destroy the Murman Railway and to arrest and shoot anybody 'directly or indirectly assisting the predatory campaign of the Anglo-French imperialists'.[12] In Baku the Armenian Dashnaks and Russian SRs were agitating for British troops to be invited from Persia to help defend the city against the advancing Turks. Clearly, that would be incompatible with the Soviet Government's policy of 'pro-German neutrality'. On that same 7 July Lenin wrote to Stalin at Tsaritsyn:

> As regards Baku, the most important thing is that you should be continuously in contact with Shaumyan, and that Shaumyan should know of the Germans' proposal, made to Ambassador Joffe in Berlin, to the effect that the Germans would agree to halt the Turks' offensive against Baku if we guaranteed the Germans part of the oil. Of course we shall agree.[13]

But the Germans did nothing to check the Turks, who eventually took Baku, almost the only effective resistance being offered by British troops belatedly called in over the opposition of Shaumyan and the other local Bolsheviks.

9 Factors in Germany's Failure in the West

Before continuing the story of developments in Russia, we should now turn to see what had happened on the Western Front to ease the German pressure on Lenin – and why.

As has been mentioned, the German morale was high at the beginning of the great offensive. The soldiers were confident that the Allies in France would collapse before their onslaught just as the Russians had. But the task before them proved to be of quite a different order. 'The troops brought over from the Eastern Front [were] unpleasantly surprised by the firmness of the British resistance.'[1] Between March and June the Germans suffered about 895 000 casualties – and still the enemy fought back.[2] General Gough, whose Fifth Army took the brunt of the initial attack, quotes a German source: 'When a great attack, from which something decisive is expected, fails hopelessly with heavy losses, the cohesion of an army is more shaken than by an unsuccessful battle.' And, from a French source: 'The morale of the German attacking divisions was very good. They were cheered by their successes at Riga and Caporetto, buoyed up by hope of victory at a single blow, an end to all their miseries. But if an instant success was not attained, their morale, thus disillusioned, would fall.'[3] German soldiers' letters home which fell into the hands of the Allies were already in June and early July saying such things as: 'All these offensives are costly and give no results, because the enemy does not yield.'[4] 'By mid-July four attacks in great strength by the Germans, first against the British then against the French, had brought then enormous losses and *no strategic gain whatever* – a demoralising situation in itself.'[5] The German General von Kuhl recalled after the war that

> both at home and also among the fighting troops, the sudden change in the summer of 1918 from the offensive, undertaken with the greatest hope of victory, to defensive action, which appeared to be hopeless in the long run, demanded the greatest efforts, and meant a gradual retreat, had a most depressing effect.[6]

The socialist Max Beer records that 'in July and August 1918 I met soldiers on leave [in Berlin] who told me that there was hardly any fight left among the troops: they said that the hope of victory had faded and that in their opinion it was time to cut the painter'.[7]

In assessing the contribution to Germany's defeat made by 'propaganda', both Bolshevik and Allied, one must start with that most effective form of it, namely, the evidence produced by plain facts. Paradoxically, the capture of Allied positions achieved in the early phases of the offensive had a demoralising effect on some of the German soldiers responsible for these achievements. For more than a year the German Army had been told that the British were close to starvation owing to the submarine blockade maintained by the Imperial navy, yet now they found in the captured British supply depots food such as *they* had not seen since early 1915.[8] Ernst Jünger describes the impression made on him and his comrades when they occupied a British trench.

> A neighbouring room [in the dugout] served as the kitchen, whose array of provisions filled us with respectful admiration. There was a whole boxful of fresh eggs. We sucked a large number on the spot, as we had long since forgotten their very name. Against the walls were stocks of tinned meat, cases of priceless thick jam, bottles of coffee-essence as well, and quantities of tomatoes and onions; in short, all that a gourmet could desire. This sight I often remembered later when we spent weeks together in the trenches on a rigid allowance of bread, washy soup and thin jam.[9]

The discovery of all this food in and behind the enemy lines not only shook the troops' confidence in what they had been told by their leaders, it also entailed delays in their advance. 'The way in which the troops stopped round food supplies, while individuals stayed behind to search houses and farms for food was a serious matter. This impaired our chances of success . . .', wrote Ludendorff himself.[10] Admiral von Müller's diary for 15 April 1918 notes that 'the offensive has come to a halt', and to this entry he later adds: 'I did not know at the time . . . what a disastrous role . . . the wine and spirits captured in the conquered territory had played.'[11] Rudolf Binding draws on his own experience in describing the hold-up in the advance due to looting of goods the Germans had not seen for years, and even opines that 'it is practically certain that the reason why we did not reach Amiens was the looting at Albert and Moreuil',[12] while the British military historian Cruttwell writes: 'The pillaging of Merville on the night of the 11th [April] undoubtedly wasted at least twelve hours of invaluable time at the very core of the battle.'[13]

The British naval blockade, by starving the Germans, undermined their resistance to the great influenza epidemic of 1918. 'Of the many causes of the German collapse, first and foremost stood the blockade', wrote General Fuller. Even with the grain of the Ukraine, supplies were short, and 'as their stomachs shrank their hearts sank'.[14] Cruttwell notes that the epidemic 'was far more severe among the Germans, owing to the poverty of their rations, than with the Entente',[15] and this view is confirmed by Jünger: although the German soldiers heard that the malady was spreading on the other side, too, 'with us the effects were worse owing to constant undernourishment'.[16]

What role was played in the slowing-down of the German offensive and in facilitating the 'turn of the tide', between the middle of July and the middle of August, by propaganda, and, in the first place, by the propaganda of the Allies? On this point it is salutary to bear in mind the words of the British historians of this subject:

> The effect of any propaganda designed to undermine the morale of the enemy invariably depends, to a considerable extent, upon the fortunes of war. Victorious troops tend to have high morale because they are victorious, regardless of any hardships which they might have to endure. They are, perhaps, most vulnerable to propaganda in the aftermath of a great offensive which has failed to bring decisive results even if it has not actually resulted in military defeat.[17]

It was, significantly, in August that the German High Command forbade their soldiers to read Allied leaflets and even offered payment for leaflets handed in.[18] It was the French victory at Villers-Cotterets on 18 July and, above all, the British break-through before Amiens on 8 August – called subsequently by Ludendorff 'the black day of the German Army in the history of this war'[19] – that finally and decisively weakened the fighting capacity of the Germans in France and created the conditions for defeatist propaganda to take effect.

But, before considering the progress of the German *débâcle* in the West between August and November, let us turn back to review developments in Russia after the liquidation of the crisis in Soviet–German relations caused by the murder of Count Mirbach.

'The black day of the German army' coincided almost exactly with the capture of Kazan by the Czechoslovaks and General Kappel's forces, and only a few days earlier the British had landed at Archangel. The danger was greater than ever before that the Bolsheviks might be driven from power by Allied and pro-Allied forces advancing from the East and North-East. What help could the Soviet Government expect to receive, in this crisis, from its German patrons? And might the latter not decide that the situation was now so highly critical, from their standpoint, that they must move in and assume direct command in Petrograd and Moscow, casting Lenin and Trotsky into the latter's famous 'dustbin of history'? But were the Germans in a position to do anything substantial in the East, either in their own immediate interest or in that of their Bolshevik clients?

Here we must consider how much hard information the Bolsheviks had, in the first half of August, concerning the actual situation and prospects on the Western Front. If they did not appreciate *to the full* how decisive a turn had actually taken place, that would not be surprising. Haig's diary for 21 August shows that Churchill, as Minister of Munitions, was still planning for a 'decisive period' in the war – in July 1919.[20] The Red Army could supply Lenin with its estimates of German capabilities and intentions, based on observation of the troops facing them along the 'screens' and on intelligence reports, and on 23 July the view taken in the Soviet Supreme War Council was that there was 'no reason to expect an offensive by Germany in the immediate future'.[21] But how significant was the information on which that view was founded? Lenin had an opportunity, on 26 July, to hear a report from within Germany itself, composed by a comrade, when the Spartakist G. Gordon (Walcher) arrived in Moscow with a letter from Clara Zetkin.[22] We know, too, that he received despatches from the Soviet ambassador in Berlin, Joffe.[23] But how well-informed was Joffe, and how sound his judgement? Perhaps the civilian politicians in Berlin were themselves not put completely in the picture at once, the terrible truth being kept from them by the military? 'In all probability', one historian opines, 'Joffe failed to provide his government with adequate information about the deteriorating situation in Germany during 1918.'[24] It was only later, in the new conjuncture of the (initialled) 'supplementary treaty', that, with confidence, *Pravda* and *Krasnaya Gazeta* could (on 17 August) assure their readers that, as a result of the Germans' setbacks on the Western Front, any active hostile measure by them was now highly unlikely.[25]

10 The Tragedy of Baku

The complicated developments in Transcaucasia in 1918 lie outside the scope of this study, except in so far as they illustrate the peculiar character of the Soviet Government's 'neutrality'. Moscow's attitude towards British help to the defenders of Baku against Turkish onslaught is comprehensible only against the background of German pressure and the Bolsheviks' readiness to submit to it. The arguments used to justify this attitude need to be compared with the secret arrangements for 'parallel actions' by the Red Army and the Germans in North Russia and on the Don, which will be dealt with later.

In Baku in April 1918 a city Soviet dominated by an alliance of Bolsheviks with Armenian nationalists was faced with the task of defending the place, with its large Armenian population and its valuable oil-wells, against an advancing Turkish army which enjoyed the support of the Muslim majority in the surrounding countryside of Azerbaijan. Baku was cut off from Soviet Russia by the Volunteer Army and the Muslim nationalists in Northern Caucasia, and could communicate with Moscow only via the Caspian Sea, through Astrakhan and Tsaritsyn. There were British troops in Iran, and the British authorities were anxious to take whatever steps should prove possible to prevent the oil of Baku from falling into the hands of the enemy. The British General, De Candolle, who had talked with the leaders of the Baku Soviet, reported on 14 April that the Bolsheviks were displaying some disposition to consider British assistance.[1] Ranald MacDonell, the British vice-consul in Baku, found that not only the Armenian nationalists, but also the leading Bolshevik, Dzhaparidze, favoured inviting British troops in to help defend the city against the Turks.[2] However, the Baku Bolsheviks, as loyal party members, had to get the approval of their top leadership before taking such a step. MacDonell reported on 29 May that Shaumyan, the chief Bolshevik in Baku, had told him 'that he cannot agree to the coming of the British force until he has obtained the authority of the Central Government'. Shaumyan asked, however, that the British troops in Iran under General Dunsterville be moved up to Enzeli, on the Caspian shore, where they would be ready to cross to Baku if and when Moscow gave the 'all clear'.[3] Two days later, though, MacDonell had to report that Shaumyan 'has told me officially that he has [received the] categorical refusal of [the] Lenin Government to allow any British force or mission to set foot on Russian territory. Shaumyan personally regrets this decision.'[4] The Baku Bolsheviks, who were evidently out of touch with thinking in Moscow, took a strongly and openly anti-German line. On the basis of a report by Shaumyan, the Baku Soviet resolved on 15 June that, 'whether in victory or in defeat, we will not give the German predators a single drop of the oil extracted by the people's labour'.[5] But Lenin telegraphed to Stalin at Tsaritsyn on 30 June that Joffe had obtained from the Germans a 'promise not to allow the Turks into Baku' – on condition that they be given supplies of oil therefrom. 'Some oil, of course, we shall give.'[6] Probably still unaware of these negotiations, Shaumyan reported to Lenin on 2 July that a couple of German officers had arrived in Baku from Tbilisi, where there was a German military mission, but he had told them to go to Moscow.[7] The contents of Lenin's telegram were passed on to Shaumyan by Stalin on 8 July: the Germans' request for oil was to be met, and, in the meantime, in his operations against the Turks, Shaumyan was to take care not to push further than Elizavetpol, so as not to encroach on territory claimed by Menshevik Georgia, whose independence was recognised by the Germans.[8]

The immediate problem, however, was not one of the forces of the 'Baku Commune' advancing too far, but of keeping the Turks out of the oil city itself. On 16 July the alliance between the Armenian nationalists and the Bolsheviks broke down. The majority in the Baku Soviet voted to call in the British. The Bolsheviks opposed the decision, and Shaumyan declared that 'an invitation to the British, while not providing us with sufficient forces to carry on the fight, can only transform Baku into a British possession'.[9] (The argument was somewhat illogical: if the British expedition was not strong enough to defend the city, Baku might well become a Turkish, or German, possession, but hardly a British one!) Although the Bolsheviks now withdrew from the city government, they remained in Baku and continued to participate in the fighting, until the British should actually arrive. They sent desperate appeals to Moscow for military help such as might enable them to save Baku by means of 'Soviet' forces alone.[10] Stalin, at Tsaritsyn, through whom Lenin communicated with Shaumyan, telegraphed Lenin on 21 July that the Baku Bolsheviks' leader had asked him for 'an urgent official communication regarding the [central] government's view. I considered it necessary to send him the following telegram' – namely, a message in which Stalin mocked the attempt of the non-Bolshevik parties in Baku 'to solve the problems of international politics in amateurish fashion', whereas the Soviet Government had declared for a policy independent of both imperialist camps.[11] Lenin confirmed Stalin's attitude on the following day.[12] On that same 22 July the Baku Bolshevik newspaper, *Bakinsky Rabochy*, evidently in a desperate attempt to make sense to its readers of the policy imposed by Moscow, wrote that the Turks were not capable of capturing the city, and the real danger came from those who were working to bring in the British.[13] Shaumyan continued to press Lenin for help, in one form or another, to get him, his comrades, and Baku itself out of their impossible situation. On 27 July he telegraphed:

> It is necessary to save Baku for Russia. Speedy aid from troops from Russia is urgently needed. I request you to take all measures for the immediate despatch of regular units. . . . I await your urgent dispositions regarding the sending of troops and your instructions regarding the decision taken to invite the British.[14]

Lenin's reply (29 July) said that any action contrary to the decision of the central government against taking help from the British 'will be considered insurrection and treason. As regards sending troops, we shall take steps, but cannot promise for certain.'[15] And on the same day, at a joint session of the All-Russian Central Executive Committee, the Moscow Soviet and the Factory Committees and Trade Unions of Moscow, after quoting a telegram from Shaumyan in which he reported that 'the British orientation has recently been making great headway among the worn-out and despairing people', he applauded the refusal of the Baku Bolsheviks to go along with it. 'This resolute rejection of any agreement whatsoever with the British and French [*sic*] imperialists was the only true course for our Baku comrades to take, for you cannot invite them without converting your independent socialist government, even though on severed territory, into a slave of imperialist war.' Proudly he added:

> We may now say that the Bolshevik, the Communist Party, is the only party which has never invited imperialists and has never entered into a rapacious alliance with them, but has only retreated before these cut-throats when they pressed too hard. . . . Our

government is not tied by a single thread to any kind of imperialist and never will be, whatever future course our revolution may take.[16]

On 9 August Lenin telegraphed to N. A. Anisimov, chairman of the Astrakhan Soviet, that 'the situation [at Baku] cannot be understood from here, and there is no possibility of giving speedy help'.[17] Meanwhile, the British expeditionary force under Dunsterville arrived in Baku, and so, as the 'explanatory' note to the above quotation from Lenin puts it, 'on 12 August a Communist conference [in Baku] took the decision to withdraw temporarily to Astrakhan, taking as many arms and as much equipment as possible'.[18] The Baku Bolsheviks informed the people of the beleaguered city that 'the proletarian socialist defence of Baku has been transformed into a war between two imperialist coalitions. There is no longer a revolutionary front in Baku, but there is an imperialist front.'[19] Then, along with the small task-force led by the Left SR G. K. Petrov which had managed to make the voyage from Astrakhan to Baku, and had participated valiantly in the defence, they tried to make their getaway – 1200 men in thirteen ships laden with guns and ammunition.[20] As is well known, they were prevented from reaching Astrakhan, brought back and imprisoned, and when, at the time of the fall of Baku, they escaped and crossed the Caspian to Krasnovodsk, they fell into the hands of anti-Bolsheviks who held them responsible for the *débâcle*, and were slaughtered.[21]

In a secret annexe to the 'supplementary treaty' between Soviet Russia and Germany signed on 27 August (of which more later), the Germans, who had promised to restrain the Turks from entering Baku, also undertook to send troops themselves to drive out the British. In fact, they did neither of these things.[22] Baku fell to the Turks in mid-September and the expected massacre of the Armenian population followed.[23]

11 'Parallel Action'

While Lenin was boasting about the Bolsheviks never having 'invited imperialists' they were in fact already contemplating an invitation to the Germans to help them solve their military problems. Paquet records that Radek was talking about German action against Murmansk as early as 24 July,[1] and on 28 July Chicherin instructed Joffe in Berlin that the hostility between the Germans and General Alekseyev's Volunteer Army should be exploited.[2] It was perhaps in preparation for the appeal about to be made to the Germans that an 'address to the toiling masses of the Allied countries' was composed on 31 July and issued on 1 August in the name of the Council of People's Commissars. The peoples of France, Britain and the other countries opposing Germany were told that if they could not defeat Germany when a large Russian army was in the field, they would hardly manage to do it now. German imperialism could be defeated only when the imperialism of *all* countries was defeated by the united attack of the world preletariat – and the road thereto lay not through continuing the war but through ending it. And, incidentally, the Allied propaganda about a German threat to the Murman Railway was false, 'because the Germans are too far away from it'.[3]

On that same day, 1 August, Lenin sent Chicherin to Helfferich, Mirbach's successor, to ask for German military action against Murmansk and against Archangel (where the British were about to land forces to help the local anti-Bolshevik and anti-German elements and, if possible, link up with the Czechoslovaks operating between the Urals and the Volga). German military action was also requested against Alekseyev's Volunteer Army. Chicherin explained that, although, 'given the state of public opinion', an open alliance between Germany and Soviet Russia was out of the question, '*de facto* parallel action' by the Germans and the Red Army was possible. As Helfferich notes in his memoirs, 'by this *démarche* the Bolshevik Government asked for our armed intervention on Great Russian territory'.[4]

The idea of such open collaboration with the Bolsheviks against what some Germans regarded as the decent elements in Russia was not at all to the liking of those Germans. Paquet wrote in his diary on 6 August, after a conversation in which Radek had spoken of the prospect of military co-operation: 'No, we don't want it to happen that, when the counter-revolution comes, we are found tied to the stinking corpse of the Bolsheviki.'[5] But the Bolsheviks' proposal offered the Germans an opportunity to play a trick on them. Helfferich himself advised 'that a show be made of complying with the Bolshevist government's plea for help, but that the troops actually march to overthrow the Bolshevists'.[6] The German command in the East had previously devised a 'contingency plan' for the seizure of Kronstadt and Petrograd, and now the Bolsheviks themselves were creating the ideal circumstances for the implementation of this plan. Movements of troops and warships could be undertaken in Karelia and the Gulf of Finland, which the Bolsheviks would imagine were part of the preparation for the 'parallel action', and by the time they realised the Germans' real intentions it would be too late.[7]

When, suddenly, Helfferich was recalled, on 7 August, the Bolsheviks did indeed wonder if some act of treachery was being prepared. On 8 August Antonov-Ovseyenko, referring to uncertainty as to the intentions of the German Government, ordered the Baltic Fleet to mine the approaches to Kronstadt, and on 9 August the commander of the northern sector of the 'screens' was warned to be on the alert for German movement in the Pskov and Narva areas. Trenches were dug in front of Petrograd and arrangements made to blow up the bridges on the railways leading to the city.[8]

However, the danger from Germany, though not wholly removed, was greatly reduced at this very moment by the action of the uniformed sections of the 'toiling masses' of Britain and France, who made 8 August 'the black day of the German army' in the West. The Crown Council at Spa to which Helfferich had been summoned discussed, for the first time, the possibility of Germany's defeat, and accepted the urgent need to curtail military commitments.[9]

Nevertheless, the Bolsheviks continued to cherish hopes that the Germans would come to their aid in the way they had proposed. On 13 August Chicherin asked for a German air bombardment of Archangel, for which the Soviet Government would provide auxiliary personnel and fuel.[10] On 18 August Uritskii, talking with the German Consul-General in Petrograd, urged that the Germans get on with their march to the White Sea without further delay. However, he added that, although it would be most convenient for the German troops to advance via Petrograd, the attitude of the workers in that city would make their passage through it too risky.

A series of meetings to persuade the workers that co-operation with Germany was unavoidable would be needed to bring about a change in the situation.[11] A Soviet military delegation led by Antonov-Ovseyenko himself went to Berlin and had talks there with the German high command, 29–31 August. They agreed to rule out the proposed offensive against Alekseyev, 'because the *matériel* for it is lacking', but the operation in North Russia should go ahead: the Bolsheviks proposed that Field-Marshal von Mackensen (of whose prowess the Russians had had direct experience in 1915) be appointed commander.[12]

In fulfilment of the plan agreed on in Berlin, a commission of three German officers set out from Pskov for Petrograd on 10 September, with a view to reconnoitring the area between Lakes Ladoga and Onega. In Petrograd they had talks with Pozern, head of the Petrograd office of the Soviets' War Commissariat, and on 14 September they proceeded to the area in question, in a special train, accompanied by General Kuznetsov and Commissar Kharitonov. Their report was dated 27 September: but that same day the German Supreme Command signalled the German HQ on the Russian front (*Oberost*) that 'Operation "Capstone" (against Petersburg)' was off, for the foreseeable future.[13] The setbacks in France had begun a process of crack-up in the Quadruple Alliance, and no adventures of that sort could be risked. General von der Goltz, who had looked forward keenly to leading his troops from Finland into Petrograd, there to put down the Bolsheviks as vigorously as he had dealt with their comrades on the other side of the Gulf, notes with regret in his memoirs that 'an opportunity of world-historical importance was passed up'.[14]

Hard upon 1 August, the date when Lenin presented the German militarists with a splendid opportunity to carry out their plan to seize Petrograd, came 7 August, when Kazan was captured by the Czechoslovaks and their Russian allies, and panic broke out in Moscow at the prospect of an enemy advance from the East upon the capital of 'Sovdepia'. Fortunately for the Bolsheviks, the next day, 8 August, turned out to be 'the black day of the German army in the West'. This meant that there could be no question of a German take-over, either in order to 'liquidate Bolshevism' or to ensure adequate resistance to the forces that threatened to re-open the Eastern Front. Not only was it the case that, in Stresemann's words, 'every last man is wanted on the Western Front',[15] there was also the point, likewise made by Stresemann on 8 August, that any other party but the Bolsheviks who might come to power in Moscow as a result of a break between the Germans and Lenin would most probably side with the Allies and re-open the Eastern Front – and that development would, given the situation in the West, be fatal for Germany.[16]

Foreign Minister Hintze replied, already on 6 August, to Ludendorff's proposal for a surprise blow at Petrograd and the overthrow of the Bolsheviks, along the same lines.

> What is it that we want in the East? The military paralysis of Russia. *That* is ensured by the Bolsheviks better and more thoroughly than by any other Russian party. . . . Helfferich reports that co-operation with other parties could be achieved only on condition that the Brest treaty be modified: above all, the Ukraine would have to be given back to Great Russia.

The Bolsheviks might indeed be a most undesirable lot, but 'we have, in general, no real choice in Russia where friends are concerned. Whoever tells Your Excellency anything different is deceiving himself.' It was an expensive luxury to bring sentiment into politics, and, 'in the situation we are in, to permit ourselves such a luxury would be irresponsible'.[17] When Hintze's rejection of his proposal reached Ludendorff, he was 'left with nothing to say – he received the document on the eve of the great military disaster of 8 August'.[18]

The changed situation on the Western Front strengthened the hand of those elements in German ruling circles who had always preferred 'peaceful penetration' of Russia to military conquest. As a Soviet historian acknowledges, the consequence of the 'black day' was that 'the influence of the Supreme Command began gradually to decline, and in the policy of the ruling circles the upper hand was gained by the supporters of continued diplomatic relations with Soviet Russia'.[19] Lenin took special steps to encourage the 'collaborationist' trend in the German leadership, offering extensive economic concessions to German capital.[20] Captain Cromie, the British naval attaché (soon to be murdered by the Bolsheviks), reported to Admiral Hall on 14 August that 'even the Western front news is withheld, by Hun order of course. The reason given to neutral enquiries as to why Allied subjects were being arrested was openly stated, that "if we don't do anything against the Allies, the Germans will do something against us".'[21] Paquet found Radek especially ingratiating in this period: 'He has tremendous respect for the German military. . . . He believes in England's downfall' (18 August).[22] In public pronouncements a picture of the situation in the West was given that would flatter the Germans (and discourage hopes in an Allied victory). Thus, Lenin, on 28 August: 'in France, the idea of "national defence" is breaking down; in Britain, the working class is denouncing the "civil truce". That means the British and French imperialists have staked their last card – and we can say with the utmost confidence that that card will be trumped (stormy applause)'.[23] Fortunately for Lenin, the real situation was, of course, quite different. This was appreciated by Joe Fineberg, a British Communist of Russian origin who had recently arrived in Moscow. On 1 August he wrote to his comrades in London:

> I was exchanging views with a comrade who had just come from Berlin, and he had come to the same conclusion as I arrived at even when I was still in England and that is that the outlook of the German and British workers is exactly the same, but at opposite poles. There is the same spirit of orderliness and lack of revolutionary feeling. There is complete war weariness in both countries, but no revolutionary initiative, and above all the fear that any action of this sort would be taken advantage of by the other side.[24]

In face of the threat from the East, the Bolsheviks needed to concentrate all their armed forces in that direction, and this they were able to do, thanks to the circumstances outlined above. On 7 August Joffe asked for a guarantee that if Red troops were withdrawn from the 'screens' the Germans would refrain from taking advantage, and Hintze assured him that there was nothing to fear on that score.[25] Accordingly, on 10 August Lenin was able to direct his Supreme War Council 'to draw up a plan for the withdrawal of the *greatest* possible number of units from the Western Front. . . . All battleworthy units should go.'[26] Next day, Sklyanskii, Trotsky's deputy, sent a directive to the War Councils of Petrograd and of the Northern and Western sectors for all combat-capable units to be sent to the Eastern Front, except for those guarding the isthmuses and on the Murmansk front. The screens facing the Germans were thus stripped of all except for the few, low-category troops needed to maintain a cordon along the demarcation line.[27]

When Trotsky learnt of Lenin's decision he asked: 'But what about the Germans?' Lenin replied: 'The Germans will not budge, they won't bother, because it is in their interest that we should finish with the Czechoslovaks.'[28] Others besides Trotsky were surprised by Lenin's confidence. A recent Soviet historian writes: 'This important decision was taken by Lenin despite the advice of the military specialists, who continued to regard the German interventionists as the main danger to Soviet Russia.'[29] General Bonch-Bruevich was removed from his post as head of the Supreme War Council on 26 August, and on 6 September this organ, which had been created primarily to direct the 'screens', was abolished.[30] Thus, Lenin was able, in August 1918, to strip his Western Front of all combat-capable troops, in order to concentrate them against the Czechoslovaks, just as Ludendorff had been able, in the winter of 1917–18, to strip his Eastern Front in preparation for the great offensive in the West. 'Instead of overthrowing the Bolsheviks at the moment of their greatest weakness, the Germans contributed substantially to saving the Soviet Government.'[31]

The Germans had, of course, to allow for the possibility of a collapse of the Red Army on the Eastern Front, when they would have no alternative but to intervene directly with such forces as they could muster. Their Foreign Office even composed a draft 'address to the Russian people', on 24 August, for use in such an eventuality. The Entente, it would be explained, in alliance with the Czechoslovaks, were trying to involve Russia in the war again. Furthermore, the Czechoslovaks stood between hungry Soviet Russia and the food of Siberia. The Germans were coming to throw out the common enemy of Germany and Russia. . . .[32] Hauschild, the German consul-general in Moscow, even entered into clandestine talks with Vatsetis, the commander of the Lettish troops whose support was vital to the Bolsheviks, with a view to ensuring that, whatever happened, the Letts would not take an anti-German line. However, although Vatsetis was friendly, he made it clear that he and his men felt they needed the support of the Bolsheviks against the Baltic Barons – Germany's protégés in Latvia – if and when they succeeded in returning home. But on 9 September Hintze sent clear instructions to Hauschild and his colleague in Petrograd, warning against intrigues with elements actually or potentially interested in changing the regime. Germany's aim in Russia, he stressed, was to postpone as long as possible any revival of the Eastern Front, and she therefore had no interest in promoting the downfall of the Soviet Government, since, as he had pointed out to Ludendorff, any other conceivable government would tear up the Brest treaty.[33] In any case, the following day, 10 September, brought the news that the Red Army had recaptured Kazan: the policy of consistent support for Lenin had paid off.

12 The Supplementary Treaty

The East-German historian Rosenfeld writes that the 'abandonment' of the Helfferich–Ludendorff plan for military action against Soviet power, after the 'black day' in the West 'meant that now the obstacle to progress in negotiations' for a supplementary treaty between Germany and Russia had been 'removed'.[1] As a Soviet historian phrases it more abstractly, 'the objective necessity for Germany to maintain peaceful relations with Soviet Russia took precedence over the subjective desires of the German politicians to bring about the downfall of Soviet power'.[2]

It was Joffe and Krassin who made the first moves towards a supplementary treaty, in early July. They urged that an agreement which would remove some of the most objectionable features of the Brest-Litovsk settlement and put German–Soviet relations on a firm basis would improve Germany's 'image' among the Russian people and even pave the way for an actual alliance.[3] The treaty was initialled on 10 August and signed on 27 August.[4] It was no accident, as the saying goes, that 27 August also saw the dissolution of the conference which had been going on in Berlin, between the Bolsheviks and the White Finns, at which the latter, hoping for German support, had been pressing for annexation to Finland of the entire Kola Peninsula and territory extending to the White Sea, Onega Bay, Lake Onega and Lake Ladoga. 'Its dissolution was the work of the Germans, who were being hard-pressed on the Western Front and who were disinclined to put up any longer with the extreme demands of the Finns.'[5] The supplementary treaty guaranteed the integrity of Soviet Russia and included a pledge by Germany to refrain from intervening 'in relations between the Russian state and its separate provinces'. German troops were to be withdrawn from Russian territory east of the Berezina, and Germany's authority in the 'occupied' provinces of Estonia and Livonia was consolidated by the renunciation of Russia's sovereignty – which meant that the Germans had the right to mobilise their populations. These provisions enabled the Germans to transfer 500 000 soldiers to the Western Front.[6] A secret clause provided that Germany might use the surviving warships of the Black Sea

Fleet, interned at Sevastopol, in any way she chose.[7] The economic articles gave Germany important advantages in the matter of war materials – in theory, at any rate. In particular, one-quarter of Baku's oil output was to be hers, though that city was still held by the British and their local allies.[8] Russia would pay to Germany an 'indemnity' of six milliard marks: Akhtamzyan points out that the importance of this sum for Germany can be gauged by the fact that, before the war, Germany's entire national income was 40 milliard marks.[9] In a secret protocol the Bolsheviks undertook to do their best to expel the British from North Russia, and if they failed, not to regard as an unfriendly act operations to the same end by the Germans, if necessary with the help of Finnish troops.[10]

Despite the burdens it placed on Russia, the supplementary treaty was not a one-sided 'Diktat', as the original peace treaty had been, but to some degree, a 'give-and-take' affair – thanks to the changed situation in the West.[11] In return for economic and financial advantages, the Germans had renounced aid to the Bolsheviks' enemies. After the treaty had been ratified, *Pravda* recognised, in passing, the fundamental condition determining Soviet Russia's relative good fortune: 'The robber claws of the Prussian brute are too deeply embedded in the Western Front. The robber has been caught in a tight spring-trap. . . .'[12] Nevertheless, had the circumstances been different, the treaty would have placed Russia in a semi-colonial relationship with Germany. 'Had the treaty itself not been nullified by Germany's subsequent collapse, Russia proper would have become an economic satellite of Germany, whatever products her ruined economy was able to export being taken by Germany as indemnity.'[13]

Joffe was pleased with the treaty, saying to Erzberger on 3 September: 'We could have obtained nothing better. Time and space are what we have gained.'[14] Nevertheless, although, as Maiskii put it, the supplementary treaty was 'the last victory of German imperialism',[15] a victory for German imperialism it was, and several historians have expressed surprise that the Bolsheviks should have conceded so much so easily. Thus, on the indemnity clause, which the Bolsheviks faithfully honoured, paying Germany 120 million gold roubles, Louis Fischer commented: 'Germany was on her last legs, and could never have forced Russia to pay. But Joffe misinformed Moscow on the strength of the Central Powers. He did not expect that their collapse was so imminent.' Without questioning Joffe's misjudgement, however, one may wonder whether these historians have perhaps underestimated the weakness of the Bolsheviks' own position in August 1918.[16]

The murder of Uritskii and the attempt on Lenin's life, at the end of August, immediately after the signing of the supplementary treaty, was answered, as is well known, by an intensification of the Red Terror, starting with the slaughter of some 500 persons who were in detention at the time of these events. Hintze sent a message of condolence to Joffe on the death of Uritskii and Lenin's wounding, but declined suggestions that he should then intervene to discourage the Bolsheviks from their 'September massacres'.[17] Furthermore, in a speech on 24 September, he declared that the excesses of the Red Terror had been exaggerated by Entente propaganda. Paquet wrote in his diary for 27 September 'the truth is (and Radek perceives this too) that we now have neither time or strength left to alter the way things are here'.[18] All this naturally had a bad effect in such anti-Bolshevik circles as had still been wavering between a pro-Allied and a pro-German 'orientation'. When news of the supplementary treaty's provisions leaked out, Germany's goose was finally cooked in the White camp. After the Volunteer Army's capture of Novorossiisk, on 26 August, there had been some friendly contacts between the German warships cruising offshore and the new masters of the port.[19] The temptation to cultivate the goodwill of the Volunteers was strong, since they were expected soon to take Grozny and Maikop, and so gain control of a source of that oil which was so badly needed by the Kaiser's war machine. But already on 11 September Admiral Hopman recorded in his diary that 'the mood in the Volunteer Army has recently become hostile to Germany'.[20] At a conference held at Ekaterinodar on 25–26 September, Alekseyev reproached a Georgian delegation for their government's co-operation with the Germans.[21] He died soon afterwards, and, according to Prince Volkonskii, 'one of Alekseyev's last orders was to forbid the crews of German vessels to land in ports occupied by the Volunteer Army, such as, for instance, Novorossiisk, Anapa, Eisk and others'.[22] The Germans had no choice now but to put up with these rebuffs. Even before they withdrew from the Taman Peninsula in October, Alekseyev's successor Denikin wrote, 'the worsened situation on the Western Front made the Germans [there] passive and compliant'.[23]

A characteristic episode of this last phase in the relations between Wilhelm's Germany and Lenin's Russia is described by G. A. Solomon, of the Soviets' trade delegation in Berlin. At a conference held in the German capital in late September and early October agreement was reached for an exchange of German coal for Russian nickel, copper, and so on, needed by the German army. Both sides were in a hurry – the Russians because the port of Petrograd would soon be closed by ice, the Germans because of the way the war was going. The coal duly arrived, and was at once placed at the disposal of the armaments factories working for the Red Army – but the German ships were returned empty by the Soviet authorities, now confident that the Germans had no capacity to hit back at them.[24]

It had taken the Bolshevik leadership a long time to appreciate fully that the danger from Germany had been removed, thanks to the Allied victories, and that they no longer needed to appease their once-great neighbour. On 11 September 'the first instalment of the Russian indemnity . . . reached Orsha, on our front line, and was taken over by the Reichsbank'.[25] This first instalment was followed by a second, and it was only at the end of October that the Soviet Government suspended payment.[26] So late as 18 September Joffe said to Nadolny that, in his opinion, Germany could hold out for perhaps another two years.[27] While reaping the benefit of the Allies' sacrifices, Lenin was not keen to shorten the period of these sacrifices by joining in the final stage of the conflict with Germany. On 22 October he warned the Ukrainian Communists against 'giving vent to their pent-up hatred and resentment by attacking the German imperialists at once . . .'.[28]

13 The End in the West

Let us now turn to examine the progress of events on the Western Front, after the 'black day', which had compelled the Germans to go so far in co-operation and conniving with the Bolsheviks. Ernst Jünger wrote that by 23 August 'there was not a man who did not know that we were on a precipitous descent . . . Every man knew that victory could no longer be ours.'[1] To withstand the hammer-blows of the Allied armies and replace the losses they inflicted, it became necessary to transfer from the occupation zone in Russia and the Ukraine as many as possible even of those low-grade troops who had been left behind in March. (A Swedish consular official had described the German soldiers in the Ukraine in June as 'practically all bespectacled Landsturm'.)[2] In September three divisions were transferred from the Ukraine to the Western Front.[3] Though service in the Ukraine had not been without its dangers, these were (especially since May) not to be compared with the prospects facing a German soldier in France at this time, and there were now 'cases every day of soldiers refusing to be sent to the Western Front'.[4] In their desperate search for manpower, the German generals resorted to re-enrolment, after long leave, of their men returned from captivity in Russia. This, Ludendorff later recalled, resulted in 'a decided deterioration in the army's morale'. The ex-prisoners-of-war 'introduced a spirit of general insubordination, showing itself particularly in definite refusal to return to the Front, thinking that, like the prisoners of war exchanged from England and France, they were under no obligation to fight any longer'.[5]

But the influence of these 'bolshy' elements ought not, in the opinion of some historians, to be exaggerated. The German Gerhard Ritter writes that it was the failure of the offensive to achieve the hoped-for results that mainly accounted for 'the slow decline of morale within the German army over the final months of war . . . Radical and subversive propaganda, mainly from soldiers who had been shipped to the dreaded Western Front from the East or from Russian prisoner-of-war camps, was by comparison of only subsidiary importance.'[6] General von Kuhl's view on anti-war agitation was that 'the effects of this pernicious activity became most apparent when there appeared to be no prospect of winning the war after the failure of our offensive in the summer of 1918'.[7] General Hoffmann wrote that 'it was only under the influence of the severe fighting during the summer of 1918 that the decay set in which brought about the disintegration in the proudest army that has ever been known in the history of the world'.[8] A historian of the German socialist movement considers that 'to the soldier at the front the superiority of enemy resources was more convincing than the influence of the [Red] agitators'.[9] In so far as 'Bolshevik propaganda' played any part in the collapse of Germany, the evidence shows that it 'only weakened German resistance after the tide of battle had turned against them': this opinion of the British historian of the Brest Treaty seems incontrovertible.[10] And the German revolution, when it came, began not in the Army but in the Navy, which had had minimal contact with the Bolsheviks! Even among the workers *out of* uniform, Tarle estimated that, though the influence of Soviet Russia was helpful to the revolutionaries in Germany, 'what was most important was something else', namely, the sense of betrayal that spread as the truth of what was happening on the Western Front came home to them.[11] Lenin's comment of 6 November on the expulsion of Joffe from Germany for alleged revolutionary propaganda is significant: 'If Germany said nothing about it before, it was because she was still strong and not afraid of us. But now, after her military collapse, she has begun to dread us.'[12]

In any case, most of the German soldiers on the Western Front fought well to the very end. They were defeated but not routed, and their retreat bore little resemblance to the collapse of the Russian army in 1917. To depict them as rotted throughout by defeatist propaganda is not only historically false but grossly unfair to a body of men who remained, on the whole, disciplined and staunch in face of overwhelming odds. The Allied victory was no walk-over, and pressure on the enemy had to be kept up to the very end. Here are a few quotations concerning the last phase of the war on the Western Front.

> The week-long battle in this key sector [east of Cambrai to the river Selle] only ended on the 24th [October] . . . In all, 24 British and two American divisions had pushed back 31 German divisions, several of whom fought stubbornly for every yard of ground . . . (During that one month of October Marshal Haig's forces suffered 120 000 battle casualties, ample evidence of the fight they still had on their hands). (G. Brook-Shepherd, *November 1918* [1981], p. 262)

> The demoralisation of the enemy would not last unless he was constantly attacked and harassed, and therefore continuous offensive action must be the role of the British armies. (General Byng's report to Haig, 8 September 1918, quoted in Jeffery Williams, *Byng of Vimy* [1983], p. 248)

> Nothing like that [meaning the French *débâcle* after Waterloo] had happened by the end of September 1918, and in fact it never happened. Right to the end, victories against the German Army were only to be won by hard fighting. (Barclay, *Armistice 1918*, p. 51)

In September, although the Germans were 'badly shaken',

> nevertheless, the hard core of the Army, notably the machine-gunners, as Hitler could claim not without an element of truth in later years, were still prepared to fight and if necessary to die for their country. (H. Essame, *The Battle for Europe, 1918* [1972], pp. 149–50)

> From the recesses of his martial spirit the German soldier summoned up reserves of courage and determination exceeding that [*sic*] of his leaders. All through October, while statesmen were discussing the Armistice preliminaries, heavy fighting continued . . . The German Army sacrificed itself heroically in the vain hope of reversing the inexorable march of fate, or at least of imposing such delays as would enable negotiators to strike a better bargain. (Terraine, *Douglas Haig*, pp. 471–2)

> As for political subversion among the German soldiers, the German Communist Ludwig Renn, after reporting 'Red' talk among his comrades when they were back in Germany in December 1918, comments: 'I had never heard such things while we were retreating through Belgium with the French close behind us. Then everybody had been against the revolutionists at the base, because on account of the confusion we were getting no food supplies'. (L. Renn, *After War* [1931], p. 10)[13]

Here, something must be said about the *Dolchstosslegende*, the legend of the stab in the back – Ludendorff's explanation of the German collapse by a betrayal of his 'undefeated' army by the people at home. This became part of the folklore of the nationalist Right in Germany: on 30 January 1941 Hitler repeated a familiar tune when he declared that 'we were never defeated by British soldiers' (Alan Bullock, *Hitler* [1962], p. 633). The phrase 'stab in the back' was inadvertently presented to the German *revanchistes* by General Sir Neil Malcolm, who headed the British Military Mission in Berlin in 1919–21. Dining with Ludendorff and listening to the German general's views on how the War ended, Malcolm asked him: 'Do you mean, General, that you were stabbed in the back?' 'Ludendorff's eyes lit up and he leapt upon the phrase like a dog on a bone. "Stabbed in the back?" he repeated. "Yes, that's it, exactly. We were stabbed in the back."'[14]

Trotsky, who might have been expected to endorse the *Dolchstosslegende*, in that, if true, it would strengthen the case for Soviet Russia's having brought about Imperial Germany's downfall through Bolshevik propaganda, nevertheless, in 1920, sneered at it. 'The bourgeoisie of the conquered countries', he wrote,

> has been embittered by defeat, the responsibility for which it is inclined to throw upon the rank and file – on the workers and peasants who proved incapable of carrying on 'the great national war' to a victorious conclusion. From this point of view, one finds very instructive those explanations, unparalleled in their effrontery, which Ludendorff gave to the Commission of the National Assembly. (Trotsky, *Terrorism and Communism* [1961; originally published in 1920], p. 67)[15]

The best discussion of the validity of the legend is to be found in the biography of Hindenburg by Margaret Goldsmith and Frederick Voigt published in 1930:

> Apparently Hindenburg came to be satisfied by the efforts made to improve the 'spirit on the home front', for on the 18th [October] he sent a circular letter to the German army commanders, impressing them that 'our united front at home [*im Innern*] can now be regarded as secured.' There had been some indiscipline in the German army hitherto, though nothing as serious as the mutinies in the French army in 1917, and there had been big strikes in Germany. But there had so far been no 'revolution from below'. The German Revolution did not break out until November – it reached Berlin on the 9th. This is extremely important, because afterwards the legend grew up – and it was adopted by all the sympathisers with the old regime, by the military leaders, and by the conservative parties – that the German army was winning the war, but that in the moment of victory it was 'stabbed in the back' by the Revolution.

Germany lost the war when her great offensives in the spring and summer of the year 1918 had failed. Before they began, Ludendorff had realised and had said that their failure would mean that all was lost. By insisting on an 'immediate armistice' he and Hindenburg not only admitted but proclaimed Germany's defeat. By declaring that the troops could retire systematically and would be able to hold the German frontiers, they acknowledged that the army was not disintegrating in a revolutionary sense (as the Russian army had disintegrated the year before). By declaring that the enemy might break through – thus consummating Germany's military defeat by military means – Hindenburg himself acknowledged that the 'home front' could be considered secure. The legend of the 'stab in the back' is therefore refuted not only by the facts but also by the testimony of the two highest possible authorities. Ludendorff, to clear his own reputation, did much to promote the legend. But Hindenburg never did – he allowed the facts to speak for themselves. (pp. 198–9)

14 Conclusion

For the Bolshevik Revolution to *succeed*, it was necessary that the Allies' Eastern Front should collapse. For the Bolshevik Revolution to *survive*, it was necessary that the Allies' Western Front should stand firm. Trotsky had warned in 1914 of the prospects before a Russia where the revolution had come about through defeat at the hands of Germany: 'the bayonets of the Hohenzollern armies would be turned on the revolution'.[1] Lenin's 'defeatism' was not, of course, designed to achieve the victory of any of the warring states. His assumption was that the defeat of one of these states would lead, first, to revolution in that particular state, and then, more or less immediately, to revolution in the state which had defeated it and in all the other warring states. But, as is well known, things did not work out like that at all. An 'uneven development' of the revolutionary process in Europe as a whole was a condition for its lasting success in Russia. This 'unevenness' had to take the form of revolution in Germany *first*, and that was what happened, but only thanks to the Allied victory in the West. As had been the case in Russia, defeat produced revolution in Germany, even if merely a revolution of the 'February' rather than the 'October' type.

Had the German offensive succeeded in 1918 and a defeated France produced an 'October'-type revolution, it is hardly likely that the Germans would have tolerated Bolshevism in Paris as they had felt obliged (so long as the Allies stood firm in France) to tolerate it in Moscow. And whereas the vastness of Russia offered *some* hope to the Bolsheviks that, even if the Germans were to occupy Petrograd and Moscow, they would still be able to hold out in the Urals or Siberia, the geographical situation in Western Europe was different. Trotsky once pointed out that if the Bolsheviks had come to power, not in Russia but in Belgium, 'We should not have had a strategy of manoeuvre, or even an army, for we should soon have ceased to be in power.'[2] And Lenin, comparing the survival of the revolution in Russia with its extinction in Hungary, 'said that Russia had been saved by her tremendous territory'.[3]

Had France gone under in 1918, it is questionable whether Britain would have been able, or America willing, to go on with the war. What would have been the consequences for Russia of a German victory? Two quotations supply the answer.

The consequences of Brest-Litovsk would have been far more serious for the Soviet regime if Germany had not been on the eve of decisive defeat on the Western front. There is no convincing evidence to show that the Bolshevik propaganda which filtered in among the German troops on the Eastern front or the surreptitious communications which passed between the Soviet Ambassador in Berlin, Joffe, and the left-wing leaders of the German Social Democrats played more than a minor role in undermining German morale and hastening the final *débâcle.* The German military empire, and the Brest-Litovsk system for East Europe, which was one of its last diplomatic achievements, were broken on the battlefields of France. Had Germany emerged from the world war victorious or at least strong enough to bargain for a free hand in the East in exchange for territorial concessions in the West, it might have gone hard with the Bolshevik Revolution. For the subsequent Allied intervention in Russia, feeble and half-hearted, intermittent and constantly thwarted by the cross-purposes and conflicting interests of its initiators, was a far less serious threat to Soviet existence than intervention of the type which Ludendorff and Hoffmann would probably have sponsored, if their system had survived the shock of military defeat. (Chamberlin, *The Russian Revolution*, vol. I, p. 412)

Compared with Brest-Litovsk, Versailles appears magnanimous. Under the Versailles [treaty] Germany had to undergo provisional eclipse as a Great Power, but Brest-Litovsk condemned Russia to dismemberment and extinction as a Great Power. Russia was dismembered in such a way that, if the Treaty had stood, she would have lost most of her industries as well as her richest agricultural region, the Ukraine, . . . and her Black Sea ports. The Baltic would have become a 'German lake' and along the eastern shores of the Baltic there would have been a series of vassal states, under German tutelage and hostile to Russia. European Russia's richest resources would have been exploited to the advantage of Germany . . . Russia herself would have ceased to be a European Power at all and would have become a crippled and mainly Asiatic state, with Germany and the German dependencies always able to paralyse her at the least sign of revolt. Her weakness would have been such that she would probably have lost Sakhalin and the Maritime Province to the Japanese. Germany's own defeat at the hands of the Western

> Powers saved Russia and the Russian Revolution. (F. A. Voigt, *Unto Caesar* [1938], p. 180)

If the efforts of the Russian army in 1914 saved France, as has been argued, especially by Russian historians, we can say that the efforts of the Western Allies in 1918 repaid that debt by saving Russia. Comparison with 1914 calls to mind an interesting point made by Dominic Lieven in his *Russia and the Origins of the First World War* (1984). Discussing the views of those Russian statesmen who, before 1914, thought that their country should refrain from participating in a war between Germany and France, he writes:

> If France fought alongside Britain, and the Germans, as was very possible, overran the former and drove the latter off the Continent, then Russia would be faced with something akin to the position in which she found herself in 1811 and 1940. She would be the single remaining truly great land power and would have on her western frontier an empire able to mobilise the resources of most of the European continent against her in the event of a conflict. (p. 82)

When he made his pact with Hitler in 1939 Stalin appears to have expected that the impending European war would not result in an '1811' situation, such as did come about in 1940, but in something like 1918 – the Allies would prevent Germany from dominating Western and Central Europe. But the fall of France ruined that scenario.[4] The situation of 1811 was re-created, and Russia had to undergo an '1812' experience once again. Fortunately, the Russia of 1941–5 was able – with help from Britain and America – to repeat the victory of 1812–14, as the Russia of 1918 would not have been.

In 1924 Trotsky said:

> It is absolutely certain that at the time of the October Revolution, if we had had to contend with a victorious Germany, with peace concluded in Europe, Germany would not have failed to crush us even if we had had 100 000, 500 000, or 3 000 000 men in the field. Neither in 1918 nor in 1919 would we have been able to find the strength to stand up against the triumphant German armies. Consequently, the struggle between the two imperialist camps was our chief line of defence.[5]

Not just the struggle between the two imperialist camps, though: the struggle in which Germany was failing to get her way and was heading for defeat. The decisive thing was – *which* camp lost. Kautsky put the matter more bluntly, as might be expected, when he wrote: 'Bolshevik Russia was not saved at that time by the revolution, but by the victory of the Entente.'[6] The gravest threat of 'intervention' that faced the Bolsheviks in 1918 was one that never materialised. The Allied 'intervention' that began during the World War and was continued for a few months thereafter was a pathetic affair compared with what a *German* onslaught could have been. Sokolnikov, writing in 1920, observed: 'True, in answer to the Brest peace the "Allied" coalition launched a new war against the proletarian republic. But, of the two enemies, this one – the Anglo-Franco-Americans – was, of course, the enemy that was less dangerous to the new Russia' – for such reasons as lack of a common frontier, disunity among the 'interventionists' (Britain v. France, America v. Japan) and so on.[7] Lenin himself had made the same point much earlier. Speaking about the Allied 'intervention' on 29 July 1918 he noted that, 'for geographical considerations alone it is clear that the form of this imperialist offensive against Russia cannot be the same as it was in the case of Germany. There are no common frontiers with Russia, as in the case of Germany; troop strength is less.'[8] Some recent Soviet writers have also acknowledged the vital difference between what happened and what might have happened but did not. V. A. Shishkin mentions that the Allied 'interventionist' forces were both much smaller than the German army of 1918 and considerably further away from Moscow and Petrograd.[9] V. G. Bryunin writes: 'Of all the capitalist countries, Germany presented at that time the greatest danger to the Soviet state, since it alone had large armed forces on our frontiers, and a renewed German offensive could have disrupted the work which had begun to lay the foundations of a socialist economy and threatened the very existence of the Soviet Republic.'[10]

The German commander in Russia, General Hoffmann, commented thus on the Allied 'intervention':

> As regards the military assistance [to the Whites] given by the Entente, one had rather the impression that the Entente contributions were on a starvation basis. The reproach that many Russians make against England in particular – that she was delighted that the war had relieved her not merely of Germany

but also of Russia, and that she was not sincerely anxious for the restoration of the old Imperial Russia – cannot be entirely dismissed.[11]

Apart from the geographical factor – expeditions to Odessa, Archangel and Vladivostok, as against attacks from Pskov and Vyborg against Petrograd – and the question of political half-heartedness, as suggested by Hoffmann, there was what might be called the chronological factor. The Allies were not in a position until the Armistice to send any large numbers of troops to Russia, but the very fact of the Armistice limited their ability to send troops. With the World War over (as they saw it), the peoples of Britain, France and the other Allied countries were unwilling to do any more fighting anywhere. 'Throughout the three years of intervention, the Allies never possessed enough troops or sufficient popular support to mount an offensive capable of crushing Soviet Russia.'[12] In relation to the Allied 'intervention', it could be said that there were as many non-Russians ('internationalists') fighting for Lenin as there were fighting against him. That would not have been the case – far from it – had the schemes of Ludendorff and Hoffmann been realised.[13]

It remains to answer a possible query as to why I have entitled this essay 'How *Haig* saved Lenin'. Why Haig? Why not some French general, or the Americans?

As regards the Americans, though their contribution to victory in the West was important, it was primarily 'psychological'. The Germans launched their offensive when they did in the hope that they could knock France and Britain out of the war before the Americans arrived in Europe in significant numbers and acquired sufficient battle-experience. In this attempt they almost succeeded. In March 1918 there were no more than seven US divisions in France, of which only one was a real fighting division.[14] And in June there were still only 17, of which seven were trained.[15] America helped to break the morale of the German High Command, *once it had failed to smash the British and French in the summer of 1918*, 'by the presence of her troops in France and by the threat of a million more to come'.[16]

As between the British and the French, the success by the latter at Villers-Cotterets on 18 July was certainly a terrible shock to the

Germans. But it was vital, after this 'second battle of the Marne', that they should not be allowed to pull themselves together as they had managed to do after the first. 'The French success of 18 July did not lead to a swift and progressive collapse of the German forces opposite the attackers . . . After the first surprise, the Germans displayed their familiar aptitude for swift reorganisation and skilful defence.'[17] The French General Mangin, the victor of 18 July, acknowledged that 'it was the British offensive of 8 August that opened Ludendorff's eyes to the situation he was in'.[18] And the French historian Renouvin concurs: 'The battle of Montdidier [as the French call the battle of Amiens] on 8 August demonstrated that the Allied high command was now capable of successfully conducting a front-breaking operation. Ludendorff knew from this moment that he was beaten.'[19] Commenting on that battle – categorised by General Fuller as 'the most decisive of the First World War'[20] – the editor of Haig's private papers sums up thus: 'The most deadly blows were dealt by the British Army, which was indeed the only really effective fighting force on the Allied side; for the Americans, though courageous, were still inexperienced and the French now in an exhausted and war-weary condition.'[21] Nor were the British outstripped in their achievements in the succeeding, final phase of the war. 'During that last "hundred days' campaign", Haig's armies took 188 700 prisoners and 2840 guns; during the same period, all the other Allies between them took 196 700 prisoners and 3775 guns.'[22] The Germans asked President Wilson on 4 October to arrange an armistice. 'On the 6th Haig was visiting Foch, and found him studying the text of the German note in a newspaper. Foch pointed to the paper: he said: "Here you have the immediate result of the British piercing the Hindenburg Line. The enemy has asked for an armistice." '[23]

The immensity of the British achievement in the final campaign of 1918 in France has in recent years received wider recognition than for a long time. For decades the influence of Lloyd George and those who took their line from him prevented proper appreciation of 'the greatest succession of victories in the British Army's whole history – victories won against the main body of the main enemy in a continental war, for the *only* time in British history.'[24] Not only did this failure to understand help the view that Imperial Germany was 'never defeated' to pass muster more easily – it also obscured an essential fact concerning the early history of Soviet Russia.

It used to be fashionable – and in some circles it still is – to disparage the historical importance of the Allied victory in 1918, and in this connection to quote Southey's well-known lines:

> 'But what good came of it at last?'
> Quoth little Peterkin.
> 'Why, that I cannot tell,' said he,
> 'But 'twas a famous victory.'

Well, without that victory we might not have had the Soviet Union which confronts us today. Whether that can be considered a 'good', in Peterkin's sense, is a contentious question.

Postscript

Much is sometimes made of the continuance of Anglo-French 'intervention' in Russia for a few months after the Armistice with Germany – as proof that there was no validity in the claim that this activity was inspired by fear of German–Bolshevik collaboration. However, apart from logistical considerations which made impossible immediate withdrawal of Allied troops from Russia after 11 November 1918, and the 'ethical' factor (how to let down gently those Russians who had been induced to rely on Allied support against the Bolsheviks), one ought not to forget that the treaty of peace was not signed by Germany until June 1919. In his introduction to the 14 November 1918 teleprinter conversation between Chicherin and Radek in Moscow and Hugo Haase in Berlin, Debo comments:

> Accustomed as we are to thinking of 11 November 1918 as marking the end of the Great War, this document reveals how precarious was the cessation of hostilities. A less moderate German government might well have chosen to explore at least the possibility of co-operation with the Bolsheviks and ultimately, as a result, the resumption of war against the Allies. (*Canadian–American Slavic Studies*, 14, no. 4 [Winter 1980], p. 520)[1]

In this talk, Chicherin tried to get the new regime in Germany to agree to joint action with the Soviets against the British fleet in the Baltic Sea, and offered to send 'French and English agitators' to Germany 'in order to conduct agitation amongst the [Allied] prisoners of war and on the Western Front' (p. 528).

In December 1918 Radek broadcast an appeal for a common struggle by Germany and Russia 'against Entente capitalism' (A. J. Ryder, *The German Revolution of 1918* [1967], pp. 174–5). On the German side, some military men proved less cautious than Haase. 'The evacuation of the Ukraine and Byelorussia after the collapse of November 1918 was deliberately carried out in such a way as to facilitate the entry of the Bolsheviks and to bring about a clash between them and the Poles. Only an energetic démarche at Berlin by the Entente in February 1919 put a stop to this policy' (Godfrey Scheele, *The Weimar Republic* [1946], p. 258). Count Ulrich von Brockdorff-Rantzau, heading the opposition in German diplomatic circles to acceptance of the peace treaty, contemplated an attempt to get rid, somehow, of the 'moderate' government: 'The point of uncertainty in his own mind seemed to be whether . . . to wait for a month or six weeks and join the Spartacists and Russians' (Count Harry Kessler, entry for 4 March 1919 in *The Diaries of a Cosmopolitan* [1971], p. 80). Testifying before the Reichstag committee which investigated the causes of Germany's defeat, the Communist deputy Arthur Rosenberg quoted, on 2 December 1925, Lenin's speech of 1 October 1918 about the possibility of a German–Soviet alliance to fight Britain and France, and observed that it was 'doubtful if a Rosa-Luxemburg government would have signed the Versailles Treaty' (*Ursachen des Zusammenbruchs*, Zweite Abteiling IV [1928], p. 98). The Comintern was already propagating the exaggerated version of the effects of the Versailles Treaty ('Germany – a slave-colony in the heart of Europe') which was to remain in its repertoire until 1933. For example, 'J.F.' (probably Joe Fineberg), in his preface (Moscow, June 1919) to the edition of M. Philips Price's *The Truth About the Allied Intervention in Russia* published by the Executive Committee of the Communist International, maintained that 'Germany is dismembered, her industry is ruined and her people doomed to generations of slavery' (p. iv).

It is well-known that Lenin, in his *'Left-Wing' Communism – An Infantile Disorder*, warned against the rigid attitude of some German Communists towards the peace treaty. That was in April 1920. Less attention has been paid to his retrospective observations, in the same passage, concerning the situation in the spring and early summer of 1919. Certainly,

> a Soviet Germany . . . would have to recognise the Treaty of Versailles for a time, and to submit to it. From this it does not follow that the Independents [Haase and Co.] – at a time when the Scheidemanns were in the government, when the Soviet Government in Hungary had not yet been overthrown, and when it was still possible that a Soviet revolution in Vienna would support Soviet Hungary – were right, under the circumstances, in putting forward the demand that the Treaty of Versailles should be signed. (*Collected Works*, 4th edn, English version, vol. 31, pp. 75–6. See also Zinoviev, 29 July 1920, at the 2nd Congress of the Comintern [*Second Congress of the Communist International: Minutes of the Proceedings*, vol. 1, 1977, p. 195].)

After the treaty had been signed, nationalist elements in Germany began at once to seek ways of frustrating its provisions, so far as possible, and the idea of co-operation with Soviet Russia soon emerged after the failure of the *Freikorps* campaign in the Baltic provinces showed that the Bolsheviks had come to stay – in Petrograd if not in Riga. In October 1919 a German aeroplane made a forced landing at Kovno. The British military mission to the Baltic States ascertained that it was carrying a mission from the Junkers firm, empowered, with the approval of the German General Staff, to negotiate the establishment of an aeroplane factory in Soviet Russia: 'as the German Government did not want to compromise itself, it gave no passes or papers to any of the party to show that they were bound for Bolshevik territory' (*Documents on German Foreign Policy*, 1st series, II [1948], pp. 44–7).

A little later, General von Seeckt, Groener's successor at the head of the Reichswehr, wrote in a memorandum dated 4 February 1920: 'Only in firm co-operation with a Great Russia will Germany have the chance of regaining her position as a world power . . . Whether we like or dislike the new Russia and her internal structure is quite immaterial' (F. L. Carsten, *The Reichswehr and German Politics* [1966], p. 68). On 7 February a Soviet agent met a high official of the German Foreign Ministry in Berlin and proposed an alliance, from which Germany could expect to get back her 'old eastern borders' (R. Himmer, 'Soviet Policy towards Germany during the Russo-Polish war, 1920', *Slavic Review*, vol. 35 [1976], no. 4, p. 671). And on 9 February Seeckt told a conference of his staff officers and departmental chiefs that if the Allies were to invade Germany to enforce their demand for the handing over of 'war criminals', the Reichswehr would conduct a fighting retreat to behind the Elbe, while in the East they would 'move against Poland and try to establish contacts with Soviet Russia, with whom, having crushed the Poles, they might march against France and Britain' (J. W. Wheeler-Bennett, *Nemesis of Power* [1954], p. 71).

The Allies did not march, but the Red Army did, and the Soviet-Polish war seemed to offer a splendid opportunity for Germany to join with the Bolsheviks in 'throwing off the chains of Versailles'. The Bolsheviks did what they could to facilitate a decision in this sense by the German authorities. Some time before 15 May a Red Army General Staff officer visited Berlin to assure the Reichswehr that the advancing Soviet forces would 'respect Germany's borders', meaning her pre-Versailles eastern frontier, and orders to this effect were indeed issued in the field (Himmer, 'Soviet Policy', p. 672; *Direktivy Glavnogo Komandovaniya*, pp. 643–4, 670). When the Red Army entered Dzialdów (Soldau), an East-Prussian town ceded to Poland by the peace treaty, they refrained from setting up a local 'soviet', handing the place over, instead, to the former German administration (C. Smogorzewski, *La Pologne restaurée* [1927], p. 152, n.2). A Berlin journalist, Rolf Brandt, reported in *Der Tag* for 19 August 1920 on his visit to Soldau a short time before, and this account was reprinted in *The Living Age* for 2 October 1920 ('With the Soviet Army'). A Red Army political officer told him:

> We have informed Moscow of our great reception here in Soldau. Moscow does not want us to mix up with the local government of former German territories. We recognise the boundaries of 1914. . . . We regard German territory as German territory . . . I do not think that the Polish Soviet Republic will lay claim to this German territory.

In conversation with some Russian soldiers, Brandt found them keen to march across Germany: 'To the Rhine against France!' He warned these hotheads that 'before the first Russian battalion reached Schneidemühl [Pila], France would seize the Ruhr', and Germany would face ruin. Brandt also visited the Red brigade headquarters at Lautenburg [Lidzbark], where the political commissar (a Lett) told him: 'These border states are ridiculous: so is this [Polish] corridor they have made. One can hardly say which is the greater folly, to try to cut Germany into two parts, or to cut Russia off from the sea.' In his speech of 19 July at the Second Congress of the Comintern, Lenin reiterated the line that Germany had been reduced by the Versailles Treaty to 'colonial dependence' (*Collected Works*, vol. 31, p. 217).

What response did the Bolsheviks get from Germany to this incitement? That there was obstruction of supplies sent across Germany from France to Poland by rail is well known, as also are the difficulties created for the Poles at Danzig (Gdansk). The Right-wing extremist Count von Reventlow recalled in 1924 that 'when the Red Army was marching on Warsaw, I was in favour of co-operating with it, from our German point of view, in order to crush the Polish state' (Ruth Fischer, *Stalin and German Communism* [1949], p. 268). There were many others like him – what Lenin called 'a strange type of Black-Hundred-revolutionary' (*Collected Works*, vol. 31, p. 276). Nevertheless, no decisive action was taken by the civil or military leadership. Clara Zetkin noted that the German bourgeois observed what was happening in Poland 'half-pleased and half-afraid' (*Reminiscences of Lenin*, 1934 New York edn, p. 18). Did they really want to see a Communist army on their eastern borders? Was bourgeois Germany strong enough to derive only benefit from a victory by the Red Army over hated Poland? This was, after all, the period of the Communist revolts which followed the Kapp Putsch. A Reichswehr Colonel, in a memorandum written in the *Truppenamt* in July, while welcoming the expected 'destruction of Poland', warned that, although 'for Germany it is essential to free herself from the chains of the Entente with the help of Soviet Russia', she must make sure that she got this result 'without falling a victim to Bolshevism' (Carsten, *The Reichswehr*, p. 69). Moreover, among the working class, outside the ranks of the Communist Party, there was no enthusiasm for actual warlike operations, since everyone realised that in the event of a German attack on Poland, France would come to the aid of her ally. 'The German Communist newspaper *Rote Fahne* adopted so militant an attitude in advocating a German alliance with Soviet Russia that it incurred the accusation from other Left parties of trying to involve the German workers in a war with France' (E. H. Carr, *German–Soviet Relations 1919–39* [1952], p. 35). However, Ruth Fischer's allegation (*Stalin and German Communism*, p. 197) that Paul Levi, then a leader of the German Communist Party, offered 'civil peace' in August 1920 to any German government that would make an alliance with Soviet Russia is apparently without foundation (letter of 12 November 1985 to me from Dr Rüdiger Zimmermann, Levi's bibliographer).

What would really have happened if Poland had collapsed in the summer of 1920 remains a matter for speculation. Might that Bolshevik–German collaboration in arms which had been canvassed in 1918 have finally come about, in the much-changed circumstances of 1920? Could Europe have been plunged once more into a major international war? Thanks to 'the miracle on the Vistula', if such a possibility existed, it never became reality.

Would Soviet Russia have been ready to ally itself with a German Government which was suppressing German Communists? In this same period it was in *de facto* alliance with Mustafa Kemal's government in Turkey, helping them to fight the Greeks, even though Kemal banned the Turkish Communist Party and had its leader murdered. If it were to be argued that, whereas Turkey was a 'colonial' country, Germany was an 'imperialist' one, so that an alliance with the former provided no valid precedent for an alliance with the latter – why, Lenin himself had answered that objection in advance, by stating that Versailles had reduced Germany to 'colonial dependence' . . .

It was appropriate that the first move from the Soviet side towards military collaboration with Germany *after* the setback suffered by the Red Army in Poland should have been made by a Turk. Enver Pasha, one of the Armenocide triumvirate who ruled Turkey in the war, had fled to Germany and made friends with General von Seeckt. He was, it seems clear, the mysterious Turk who was reported to be among the passengers in that German aeroplane which came down at Kovno in October 1919. After he had, at last, got to Moscow, Enver wrote to Seeckt, on 26 August 1920, about a talk he had had with Sklyanskii, Trotsky's deputy: 'A party here [perhaps "faction" would have been a better term? – B.P.], which possesses real power, and to which Trotsky belongs, favours an understanding with Germany.' This group would be prepared to 'recognise the old German frontier of 1914' (Carsten, *The Reichswehr*, pp. 70–1).

In view of the Red Army's poor showing in Poland, Seeckt was, naturally, not enthusiastic about this Soviet approach – which, in any case, came unofficially and from what Enver admitted was only one 'tendency' in the Soviet leadership. However, in the spring of 1921, 'Lenin applied formally to the German Government for assistance in the reorganisation of the Red Army' (Otto Gessler, German Minister of Defence, testified to this before the Foreign Affairs Committee of the Reichstag on 24 February 1927: Wheeler-Bennett, *Nemesis of Power*, p. 127). And so began that semi-secret collaboration between the Reichswehr and the Red Army, in the spheres of training and the provision of weapons, which, while doubtless helping to build the Soviet forces, certainly created some of the essential pre-requisites for the rapid and formidable expansion of *Germany's* forces after Hitler's accession to power in 1933: for the formation of that mighty iron fist which struck at Russia in 1941.

Map 1: Russia 1918

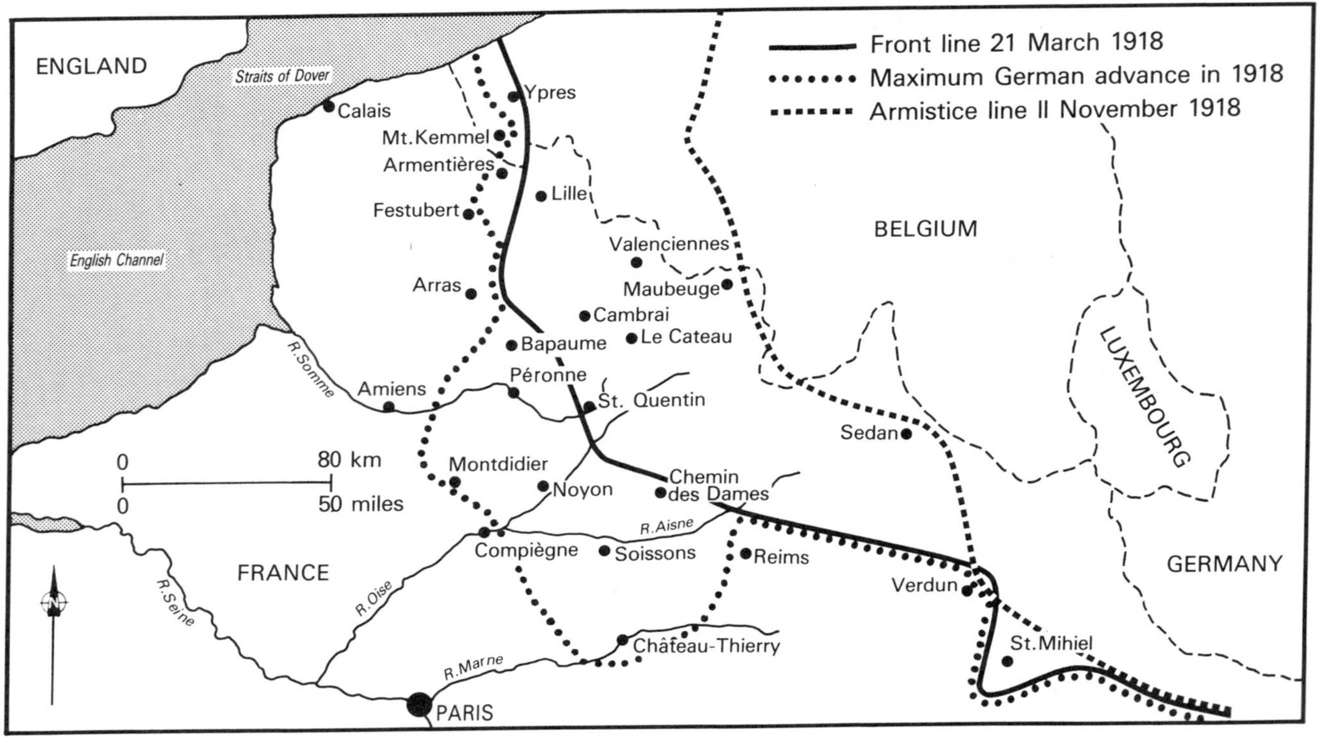

Map 2: The Western Front 1918

Select Chronology of Events in 1918

FEBRUARY

10 Trotsky at Brest-Litovsk declares: 'Neither peace nor war'.
18 German and Turkish offensive against Soviet Russia begins.
21 Germans take Minsk.
24 Germans take Pskov and Zhitomir.

MARCH

1 Germans enter Kiev.
3 Peace treaty signed at Brest-Litovsk.
4 Germans take Narva.
5 Soviet decree establishing 'screens'.
6 British troops land at Murmansk.
8 Trotsky becomes People's Commissar for Military and Naval Affairs.
9 Soviet Government moves from Petrograd to Moscow.
13 Germans and Austrians take Odessa.
16 Congress of Soviets ratifies peace treaty.
17 Germans take Nikolayev.
19 Germans and Austrians take Kherson.
20 Germans and Austrians in occupation of all Right-bank Ukraine.
21 German offensive begins on Western Front.
22 Germans break British line west of St Quentin.
23 German long-range gun shells Paris.
24 Germans take Bapaume and Péronne.
25 Germans take Noyon.
27 Germans take Montdidier.
29 Germans take Poltava.

APRIL

3 Germans land in Finland.
4 British hold their line at Festubert.
8 Germans take Kharkov.
12 German air-raid on Paris; Haig's 'Backs to the wall' order.
14 Germans enter Helsingfors (Helsinki); Foch made Allied Commander-in-Chief.
19 Germans enter Crimea.
25 Germans take Mount Kemmel.
29 Germans overthrow Rada, instal Skoropadskii as 'Hetman' of Ukraine.
30 Germans take Sevastopol.

MAY

1 Germans take Taganrog.
4 Soviet Russia and Ukraine sign armistice.
7 Germany and Romania sign Treaty of Bucharest.
8 Germans take Rostov-on-Don.
25 Czechoslovak revolt begins.
27 Germans take Chemin-des-Dames.
28 Germans cross River Aisne.
29 Czechoslovaks take Penza; Germans take Soissons.
31 Germans reach River Marne.

JUNE

4 Germans take Château-Thierry.
6 German ultimatum regarding Black Sea Fleet.
8 Czechoslovaks take Samara (Kuibyshev).
12 Germans enter Tiflis (Tbilisi).
18 Black Sea Fleet ships scuttled at Novorossiisk.
23 More British troops land at Murmansk.
24 Kühlmann admits war cannot be won by military means.
28 Soviet Government's decree nationalising many enterprises.

JULY

2 German leaders discuss Russian question at Spa.
6 German Ambassador Count Mirbach murdered in Moscow; Czechoslovaks take Ufa.
10 German Chancellor Kühlmann resigns.
10–11 Mutiny by Soviet Eastern Front Commander Muravyev: replaced by Vatsetis.
16 Tsar and family murdered at Ekaterinburg (Sverdlovsk).
18 Allied counter-offensive begins in France.
21 Allies recapture Château-Thierry.
22 Czechoslovaks take Simbirsk (Ulyanovsk).
24 Helfferich appointed to succeed Mirbach.
25 Czechoslovaks take Ekaterinburg (Sverdlovsk).
30 Eichhorn, German Commander-in-Chief in Ukraine, murdered.

AUGUST

1 Soviet Government proposes 'parallel action' with Germans against British.
2 Allies recapture Soissons; British land at Archangel.
4 British land at Baku.
7 Czechoslovaks take Kazan; Germany reassures Soviet Government regarding transfer of troops.
8 Battle of Amiens; 'Black Day of the German Army'.
10 Allies recapture Montdidier.
15 Last German artillery bombardment of Paris.
26 Volunteer Army takes Novorossiisk.
27 'Supplementary treaty' signed by Soviet Russia and Germany.
29 Allies recapture Noyon and Bapaume.
29–31 Military conference between Germans and Soviets in Berlin.
30 Attempt on Lenin's life.
31 Attack on British Embassy: Cromie killed; Allies recapture Mount Kemmel.

SEPTEMBER

1 Allies recapture Péronne.
2 Soviet Russia proclaimed 'an armed camp'.
7 First instalment of 'indemnity' to Germany paid by Soviet Russia.
10 Soviet troops recapture Kazan.
11 'Screens' liquidated and troops redeployed.
12 Battle for Hindenburg Line begins; Soviet troops recapture Simbirsk (Ulyanovsk).
14 Turks take Baku.
29 Hindenburg Line pierced between Cambrai and St Quentin; Hindenburg urges German Government to seek peace talks.

OCTOBER

2 Allies recapture St Quentin.
3 Allies recapture Armentières; Soviet troops recapture Syzran.
4 German Government asks for armistice.
7 Soviet troops recapture Samara (Kuibyshev).
9 Allies recapture Cambrai.
10 Allies recapture Le Cateau.
17 Allies recapture Lille.
20 Belgian coast cleared.
26 Ludendorff resigns.
28 Sailors' mutiny begins at Kiel.

NOVEMBER

3 Allies recapture Valenciennes.
6 Allies recapture Sedan.
8 Allies recapture Maubeuge.
9 Kaiser Wilhelm II abdicates; German Republic proclaimed.
11 Armistice in the West.
13 Soviet Government annuls Treaty of Brest-Litovsk.
21 Soviet troops enter Polotsk.
25 Soviet troops enter Pskov.
28 Soviet troops enter Narva and Bobruisk.

DECEMBER

2 Soviet troops enter Borisov.
9 Soviet troops enter Dvinsk (Daugavpils).
10 Soviet troops enter Minsk.

Notes and References

1 A SOVIET MYTH

1. In another place (*Ruskii front pervoi mirovoi voiny* [1976], p. 370) Rostunov admits that it was Allied pressure in the West that kept Petrograd free for the Bolsheviks to stage their 'October Revolution' in, when he writes: 'After their capture of Riga the German high command was obliged to transfer some divisions of the Eighth Army to the Western Front and Italy. Otherwise, nothing would have prevented them from advancing on Petrograd.'
2. Public Record Office, FO 371/3310/6596.
3. René Marchand, *Pourquoi je me suis rallié à la formule de la révolution sociale* (1919) p. 24. (Of the two Tsarist generals mentioned, the former was murdered by the Bolsheviks and the latter entered their service.)
4. Ministère des Affaires Etrangères (Paris), Guerre, Russie, Action des Alliés, 32/119 (quoted by R. K. Debo, 'Litvinov and Kamenev – Ambassadors Extraordinary', *Slavic Review*, vol. XXXIV, no. 3 (September 1975), p. 476).
5. Lenin, speech on 28 August 1918, in *Collected Works*, 4th edn, English version, vol. 28, p. 86.
6. Ibid., vol. 27, p. 479.
7. Ibid., vol. 28, p. 149.
8. 25 December 1918: ibid., vol. 28, p. 376.
9. *Bolshevik Propaganda. Hearings before a Subcommittee of the Committee of the Judiciary. United States Senate, 65th Congress.* Published as Senate Document no. 62, 66th Congress, First Session, vol. 3, Washington (DC), 1919, p. 630.
10. Ibid., p. 747.
11. M. P. Price, *The Origin and Growth of the Russian Soviets* (1919), p. 8.
12. Honourable mention should be made of the article entitled 'The "rejuvenation" of a legend', by Major-General A. Shcherbakov, in *Voenno-istoricheskii zhurnal*, no. 8 of 1964, in which he writes, with soldierly bluntness: 'The German militarists suffered defeat on the field of battle. . . . The imperialist war was ended not by a revolt of the working class but by the complete military defeat and bankruptcy of German militarism' (p. 52). In this case, concern to refute the 'stab-in-the-back' propaganda of German nationalists has caused justice to be done to the Anglo-French forces – a 'positive' side-effect of the Soviet obsession with 'revanchism'.

2 RUSSIA'S DEFECTION AND THE WESTERN FRONT

1. Writers who denigrate Haig's strategy, in connection with the Somme battle, not only overlook the need to take pressure off our French allies

at Verdun but also fail to note the 'wearing-down' effect on the German Army which prepared the way for its failure in 1918 (see General Lord Rawlinson, foreword to General Sir Archibald Montgomery's *The Story of the Fourth Army* [1920], p. vii). Commenting on the spate of 'war books' in 1928–31, Correlli Barnett makes the same point. None of the novelists and memoirists in question 'seems to see any connexion between the Allies' eventual victory in 1918 and the terrible battles that went before. How do they think the German army grew so weak?' (*A Military Historian's View of the Great War*, Royal Society of Literature, Essays, New Series, vol. 36 [1970], p. 16). The enemy's leaders had no doubts on this score. Ludendorff wrote of the consequences for his men of the Somme battle: 'The Army had been fought to a standstill and was utterly worn out' (*My War Memories* [1919], vol. I, p. 304). Hindenburg noted, regarding the German forces after mid-1916: 'The military machine with which we were now working was not to be compared with those of 1914 and 1915, or indeed with that of the opening months of 1916' (*Out of My Life* [1920], pp. 262–3).

2. General Max Hoffmann, *War Diaries and Other Papers* (1929), vol. 2, p. 190.
3. That is, in *Histoire de la Guerre Mondiale*, vol. 4, *Foch et la victoire des Alliés, 1918* (1936).
4. W. Steglich, *Die Friedenspolitik der Mittelmächte 1917–1918*, vol. I (1964), p. 248. Cf. Hoffmann, *War Diaries and Other Papers*, vol. 2, p. 194.
5. Cyril Falls, *The First World War* (1960), p. 315.
6. Published originally in German, this book was translated into English and enjoyed, in its time, great authority in Communist and fellow-travelling circles. See the entries in Philip Grierson's *Books on Soviet Russia, 1917–42* (1943), pp. 10, 38.
7. Golo Mann, *History of Germany* (1972), p. 326. Cf. also: 'Immediately following the negotiations at Brest-Litovsk, . . . the old chauvinist tendencies came to the fore again' in Germany (A. K. Bazarevskii, *Mirovaya voina 1914–1918 gg. Kampaniya 1918 goda vo Frantsii i Bel'gii* [1927], vol. 1, p. 88); and: 'The German people had not yet by any means buried their hopes for victory. On the contrary, the peace treaties that had been concluded in the East served as a promising augury of ultimate success in the war' (Gerhard Ritter, *The Sword and the Sceptre*, vol. 4 [1973], p. 232).
8. *Ursachen des Zusammenbruchs*, Reichstag, 12 Ausschuss, Beilage (1923), p. 216.
9. Ernst Jünger, *Storm of Steel* (1929), p. 251.
10. M. Middlebrook, *The Kaiser's Battle* (1978), p. 63.
11. W. Baumgart (ed.), *Von Brest-Litovsk zur deutschen November-revolution* (1971: the diaries of Alfons Paquet, General Wilhelm Groener and Admiral Albert Hopman), p. 433.
12. F. S. Oliver, *The Anvil of War* (1936), p. 318, n.
13. J. E. Valluy, *La Première Guerre Mondiale* (1968), vol. 2, p. 200.
14. F. I. Notovich, *Razgrom germanskoi armii v 1918 g.* (1941), p. 9.

15. C. N. Barclay, *Armistice 1918* (1968), p. 14; G. Brook-Shepherd, *November 1918* (1981), p. 23.
16. Lloyd Griscom, *Diplomatically Speaking* (1941), pp. 398, 400. 'The French almost decided, at one stage, to break contact with the British and pull their forces back to protect Paris' (Middlebrook, *The Kaiser's Battle*, p. 346). 'Even on the eve of the first battle of the Marne, Germany had never seemed to be so close to final victory' (Louis Madelin, *La Bataille de France* [1920], p. 356). General Hoffmann noted in his diary on 17 June: 'The position in the West is good. The French are in a complete quandary . . . The tone of the French newspapers is already different from what it has been in the last four years' (Hoffmann, *War Diaries and Other Papers*, vol. 1, p. 221).
17. John Terraine, *Douglas Haig* (1963), p. 433. To this grim mood on the British side corresponded a justified exultation among the Germans. 'As the first offensive drove the British back upon Amiens, a wave of enthusiasm swept over Germany. The morale of the advancing army was at its height, and the ranks, stiffened by the veteran eastern troops, were confident of ultimate success' (R. H. Lutz, *The German Revolution* [1922], p. 8). Herbert Sulzbach, then serving on the Western Front, wrote in his diary on 7 April 1918, after learning of the Germans' victory in Finland: 'We have troops all over the world! And wherever they are, they are winning!' (*With the German Guns* [1973], p. 163).
18. Theses on the Current Situation, in the Moscow *Kommunist*, no. 1, 20 April 1918. The Brest-Litovsk terms showed up the unrealism of Lenin's argument in 1916, when he wrote: 'What is the present war being fought over? . . . The Germans' purpose – and, more important, the policy that would bring it to realisation if they were to win . . . is definitely not to bring the French or the Russians under foreign domination' (*Collected Works*, vol. 23, pp. 33–4). Tarle described, in 1928, how the first effect of the news of peace in the East, among workers in the West, was to make them wish that the same should happen on their fronts: but how, when they learnt of the terms of the treaty, their mood changed, and the imperialists of the Entente could once more demand of their war-weary peoples a fight to the bitter end (E. V. Tarle, *Evropa y epokhu imperializma*, 1928, in *Sochineniya*, vol. 5 [1958], pp. 389–90). It was all very different from the scenario prophesied by Lenin to A. G. Shlyapnikov on 23 August 1915. Welcoming the misfortunes suffered by his country's army, the Bolshevik leader then wrote:

> The military reverses are helping to shake the foundations of Tsarism and facilitating an alliance of the revolutionary workers of all countries. People say: what will 'you' do if 'you', the revolutionaries, defeat Tsarism? I reply: (1) our victory will fan the flames of the 'Left' movement in Germany a hundredfold; (2) if 'we' defeated Tsarism completely, we would propose peace to all the belligerent powers on democratic terms, and if this were rejected, we would conduct a *revolutionary* war. (*Collected Works*, vol. 35, pp. 204–5)

19. *Spartakusbrief* no. 11, September 1918, 'The Russian Tragedy', in Rosa Luxemburg, *Selected Political Writings*, ed. R. Looker (1972), p. 239.

Karl Liebknecht 'recognised that the Bolshevik peace policy had become "a saving act for German imperialism . . . quite against the wishes of our Russian friends" ' (H. Trotnow, *Karl Liebknecht* [1984], p. 194).

20. *Bolshevik Propaganda*, p. 388. Cf. D. W. Morgan, *The Socialist Left and the German Revolution* (1975):

> On November 27 [1917] the Soviet Government announced that it would seek a separate peace with Germany. This disconcerting news strained the radical socialists' sympathy; it would be hard to call on the German workers to launch an attack on the German imperial regime if even Bolshevik Russia were to give up the struggle. (p. 87)

And, after the January 1918 strike,

> while the rebels were recuperating, Germany's war position took an apparent turn for the better. The settlement with Russia became an accomplished fact, which was a general source of relief. And the successes achieved by the German offensive on the Western front began to mount up, giving rise to hopes that the war might finally be won. The spirit that brings political mass actions did not rise again until October, when the obvious military and political crisis came. (p. 91)

Cf. also A. J. Ryder, *The German Revolution of 1918* (1967), about the mood in Germany after Brest-Litovsk: 'In April [1918] . . . under the influence of Ludendorff's victories in the West, *Vorwärts* [the newspaper of the Social-Democrats] wrote of a complete and imminent German victory' (p. 115). 'The German revolution would never have taken place but for military defeat, and very little of the revolutionary spirit was to be observed among civilians or soldiers during the next few months, when Ludendorff's initially successful offensive revived hopes of victory' (p. 118).

21. L. D. Trotsky, *The War and the International*, reprinted in 1918 as *The Bolsheviki and World Peace*, pp. 31–2.

3 FEBRUARY 1918 IN RUSSIA

1. Trotsky, *The Bolsheviki and World Peace*, p. 87. Cf. Lenin, wise after the event, on 24 February 1918, speaking of the German Army: 'Before us is the oppressor with his knee on our chest' (*Collected Works*, vol. 27, p. 46).
2. Lenin, *Collected Works*, vol. 27, p. 63. A little later Lenin described the situation even more frankly. 'Everyone of integrity who came from the front said that, had the Germans made the slightest attack, we should have perished inevitably and absolutely. We should have fallen prey to the enemy within a few days' (7 March 1918: *Collected Works*, vol. 27, p. 103). Contrast with this the picture drawn by that 'loyal Leninist' Jacques Sadoul in his *Naissance de l'URSS* (1946, p. 299). According to him (and he was in Russia at the time!), the Red Guards 'broke all the onslaughts by the experienced troops of German imperialism, who were eventually compelled to retreat. Red Army Day

is celebrated every year on 23 February, the anniversary of this wonderful victory . . . The German Government, now surprised and worried, agreed to make peace.' The true reason for the Germans' cessation of their advance is acknowledged by A. I. Cherepanov, in *Pod Pskovom i Narvoi* (1963, p. 138): 'An advance on Petrograd and Moscow and into the heart of Russia would have required large forces, and these were tied up in the tense struggle on the Western Front.'

3. Louis de Robien, *Journal d'un Diplomate en Russie* (1967), pp. 257–8.
4. C. Anet, *La Révolution russe*, vol. 4 (1919), p. 86.
5. A. L. Fraiman, *Revolyutsionnaya zashchita Petrograda v fevrale-marte 1918 g.* (1964), p. 97.
6. Ibid., pp. 245, and 251. David Mandel, in *The Petrograd Workers and the Soviet Seizure of Power* (1984), describes how, when Pskov fell ('only 250 km. from Petrograd') many of the workers in the capital demanded 'severance pay' before fleeing into the interior (pp. 388–98). Korablev, reviewing Fraiman's book in *Voenno-istoricheskii zhurnal*, no. 11 of 1964, considers that the figure of 38 000 volunteers in Petrograd is an underestimate, some factories having been left out of account. But he admits that the volunteer units, although 'in many places they delayed the advance of the German divisions, . . . could not halt their advance, for the contending forces were too unequal' (p. 93).
7. I. M. Sverdlov, *Izbranniye proizvedeniya*, vol. 2 (1959), pp. 138–9, 152. The Bolshevised Lettish Riflemen took the same line, namely, that the precious few reliable fighters for the principles of October must not be wasted in battle with the Germans. They 'retreated at full speed, barely staying ahead' of the advancing enemy. 'Resistance was almost universally condemned to be useless, and the official organs of the Strelki [Riflemen] recommended retreat so that the Strelki regiments could be preserved for struggle against counter-revolution' (A. Ezergailis, *The Latvian Impact on the Russian Revolution* [1983], pp. 353, 354). Another factor of a political order which the Bolsheviks had to take into account in making their military calculations was that the few units of the old army which had retained their morale and could have been used to oppose the Germans included some that were anti-Bolshevik (for example, the Preobrazhenskii Regiment) and which they therefore preferred to demobilise (N. Rutych, *Le Parti communiste au pouvoir en URSS, 1917–1960* [1961], p. 114; L. Schapiro, *The Origin of the Communist Autocracy* [2nd edn, 1977], p. 105).
8. S. T. Possony, in *Lenin: the Compulsive Revolutionary* (1964), pp. 265 seq., concurs with Steinberg on this point. Yu. G. Fel'shtinskii, in *Bol'shevski i levye esery okt. 1917–iyul' 1918* (1985), also takes the view that, in this crisis, Lenin 'sowed panic' for special political motives (p. 112).

   Voenno-istoricheskii zhurnal published in its no. 12 of 1964 a manuscript by Krylenko describing the military situation in February 1918 ('The death of the old army') which had been found in Podvoiskii's archives. This work had been prepared for publication, but the arrest (in 1938) of the former Commander-in-Chief had supervened. Krylenko recalled the effect of an order dated 23 December 1917 which appealed to all sincere revolutionary soldiers of the old army to enlist in the new volunteer army which was to be formed, and mentioned the possibility of a 'holy revolutionary war'. 'From the moment that this order reached the front there began a break-up which it was impossible to prevent'. Panic seized whole units. The soldiers had expected from the new government peace, not a new war (p. 52). And when the Germans advanced, the Russian troops ran, 'sweeping aside as they went the units which had been sent from the centre, having been hastily mobilised inside the country'. The result was that, for the moment, 'all the work done to organise a Red Army was brought to naught' (p. 55).

Because 23 February is celebrated in the USSR as Army Day, Western writers frequently state that this was the date in 1918 when the Red Army was founded (for example, E. H. Carr, in *The Russian Revolution* [1979], p. 11: 'On February 23 1918, . . . the Red Army came into being'). In fact, the decree establishing the Red Army had been issued in January, and, as Voroshilov acknowledged in an article in *Pravda* of 5 March 1933, the choice of a date for the commemoration, in 1919, was 'rather accidental'. In 1938 Stalin, in his *Short Course of History of the CPSU (B)*, pronounced that 'at Narva and Pskov the German invaders met with a resolute repulse. Their advance on Petrograd was checked. February 23 – the day the forces of German imperialism were repulsed – is regarded as the birthday of the Red Army' (English-language edn [1939], p. 217). All this was de-bunked by Major-General S. F. Naida in an answer to a reader's question published in *Voenno-istoricheskii zhurnal*, no. 5 of 1964: as he wrote, 'on 23 February 1918 there were no battles at Pskov or, still less, at Narva'.

9. Lenin, *Collected Works*, vol. 27, p. 63; Fraiman, *Revolyutsionnaya zaschita Petrograda v fevrale–marte 1918 g.* (1964), p. 112, n. 211.
10. *The Bolsheviks and the October Revolution: Central Committee Minutes for August 1917–February 1918* (1974), pp. 212–15.
11. Lenin, *Collected Works*, vol. 28, p. 67.
12. Jean Delmas, 'Une mission militaire française à Petrograd après la Révolution d'Octobre', in *Revue de Défense Nationale*, June 1966, p. 1089.
13. FO 371/3284, p. 546.
14. *Canadian–American Slavic Studies*, no. 4 of 1974, p. 554. In *The Russian Revolution* (1979), E. H. Carr wrote (p. 10) that during the negotiations at Brest-Litovsk, 'informal – *and fruitless* [my emphasis, B.P.] – approaches were made to British, French and American representatives in the hope of soliciting Western aid against the Germans'. Yet, from his service at the Foreign Office, Carr must have known better than most how unfair that statement was.

    The British officer George Hill organised, by agreement with Trotsky, sabotage actions to obstruct the German advance into the Ukraine, blowing up gasometers and wrecking railway lines (George Hill, *Go Spy The Land* [1932], p. 230, and *Dreaded Hour* [1936], p. 5). The French Captain Bordes blew up two bridges west of Krivoy Rog. French personnel working in the mines and factories of the Donbas arranged the evacuation to Tsaritsyn of quantities of explosives and machinery (Valluy, *La Première Guerre Mondiale*, vol. 2, p. 149: D. Venner, *Histoire de l'armée rouge* [1981], vol. 1, pp. 150–1).

The question of Allied aid to the Bolsheviks against Germany in this period is usefully discussed in General H. A. Niessel's *Le Triomphe des bolcheviks et la paix de Brest-Litovsk* (1940), especially pp. 279–81 and 342. See also M. J. Carley's article in the *Journal of Modern History*, vol. XLVIII (1976), no. 3, pp. 418–19; R. K. Debo, *Revolution and Survival* (1979), pp. 138–42; and J. F. N. Bradley, *Allied Intervention in Russia* (1968), p. 20.

15. The Soviet historian V. S. Vasyukov sensibly observed that ('even if the Allies had really intended to give Soviet Russia real help') in February 1918, such help – by which he means the despatch of an expeditionary force – could not have been decisive. The outcome of the struggle was bound to be decided within a week or two, at most, since the Germans were already so close to Petrograd, and the Allies, with the best will in the world, could not have got their troops in position to defend the capital before two or three months had passed (*Predistoriya interventsii* [1968], p. 281).

4 BREST-LITOVSK AND AFTER

1. On 9 April 1918, Woodhouse, the British consul in Petrograd, informed the Foreign Office: 'Am assured that already over 200 000 rifles and 15 million rounds ammunition have been brought away [from Archangel] and sold to Germany' (FO 371/3305/65252).
2. M. S. Kedrov, *Bez bol'shevistskogo rukovodstva* (1930), p. 28. Kedrov denounces Trotsky for sending this order, and subsequent Soviet writers have repeated his denunciation, claiming that he acted without the approval of Lenin, though no proof of this is ever given. Trotsky wrote in *Izvestiya*, 4 July 1918, that the measures he then took were 'completely in accordance with the instructions I received from the Council of People's Commissars and, in particular, from the Commissariat for Foreign Affairs' (*How The Revolution Armed*, English translation, vol. I [1979], p. 262), but this was dismissed as a 'lying, pettifogging statement' by N. A. Kornatovskii in *Krasnaya Letopis'*, no. 3(36), (1930), p. 35.
3. Lockhart to Foreign Office, 2 May 1918 (FO 371/3507/84551).
4. FO 371/3307/81518. Morgan Philips Price reported in the *Manchester Guardian* of 11 May that the Finnish Communist Tokoi, recently arrived in Moscow, had told him that 3000 Finnish Red Guards had reached Kandalaksha. 'The ground is now well prepared for co-operation by the English and American democracies with the revolutionary forces of Russia and Finland . . . .' General Sir H. E. Blumberg, in *Britain's Sea Soldiers: A History of the Royal Marines 1914–1919* (1927), describes (pp. 195–6) the collaboration between British and Red Finnish forces in fighting against the White Finns on the approaches to Pechenga.

5. FO 371/3307/90360.
6. FO 371/3307/93884.
7. R. H. Ullman, *Anglo-Soviet Relations, 1917–1921*, vol. I, *Intervention and the War* (1961), pp. 179–80.
8. FO 371/3307/93608.
9. M. J. Carley, 'The origins of the French intervention in the Russian civil war', in *Journal of Modern History*, vol. XLVIII (1976), no. 3, p. 420.
10. FO 371/3320/67490.
11. FO 371/3327/67933. See also J. Noulens, *Mon Ambassade en Russie* (1933), vol. II, pp. 55–8, 67–71, and Carley, 'The origins of the French intervention', pp. 423–6.
12. 'The Historical Importance of the October Revolution', in M. N. Pokrovskii, *Russia in World History: Selected Essays* (1970), p. 209.

    Many officers of the old army were lured into service with the Red Army by the belief that it would be used against Germany, and their first months in the new army were indeed spent in the 'screens': when, later, they found they were required to wage a civil war, some crossed over to the Whites, others committed suicide, and yet others decided to carry on – either from inertia, from fear of the consequences of defection, or because they had by then accepted that the Bolshevik regime was, 'after all', the *de facto* Government of Russia. (Cf. Yu. Korablev, *V. I. Lenin i sozdanie Krasnoi Armii* [1970], p. 240).
13. FO 371/3285/61467 (p. 268).
14. J. Sadoul, *Notes sur la Révolution bolchevique* (1971; originally published in 1919), p. 330.
15. Trotsky, 16 June 1918, quoted in A. L. P. Dennis, *The Foreign Policies of Soviet Russia* (1924), p. 286. See also Trotsky's article of 22 June, in *How The Revolution Armed*, vol. I, p. 260. Rosa Luxemburg commented from inside Germany:

    > Trotsky is supposed to have said that if Russia had to choose between Japanese and German occupation, she would choose the latter, since Germany was far more ripe for revolution than Japan . . . Trotsky's reasoning is completely wrong, however, since the prospects and possibilities of a revolution in Germany are dimmed each time German militarism is strengthened or gains a victory. (*Selected Political Writings*, p. 240)

    Stalin's speech of 2 September 1945 appeared in *Soviet Weekly*, 4 September 1945. (It was in this speech that Stalin spoke of Japan having invaded the Russian Far East in 1918 'taking advantage of the then hostile attitude of Britain, France and the USA'. Until then, the USA had been presented in the USSR as having *opposed* Japanese intervention, and in 1933, for this reason, all claims against the USA in connection with intervention had been waived.) For the Bolsheviks' cheering-on of the 'progressive bourgeoisie' of Japan in their war against Russia, see Lenin's articles 'The Fall of Port Arthur', 'European Capital and the Autocracy' and 'The Débâcle', in vol. 8 of the *Collected Works*.
16. Lenin, *Collected Works*, vol. 26, pp. 445–6.

17. Ibid., vol. 27, p. 28.
18. Ibid., vol. 44, p. 67.
19. Ibid., vol. 27, p. 39.
20. W. Hard, *Raymond Robins' Own Story* (1920), pp. 151–2; see also W. P. and Z. K. Coates, *Armed Intervention in Russia* (1935), p. 65.
21. Lenin, *Collected Works*, vol. 27, p. 77.
22. G. F. Kennan, *Soviet–American Relations, 1917–1920*, vol. I, *Russia Leaves The War* (1956), pp. 500–5, 516.
23. Kennan, *Soviet–American Relations, 1917–1920*, vol. II, *The Decision to Intervene* (1958), pp. 134–5.
24. A. B. Ulam, *Expansion and Coexistence* (1968), p. 70. Alexandra Kollontai 'spoke of a conspiracy of the British, the French and the Germans, while those nations were slaughtering each other in France' (Barbara Evans Clements, *Bolshevik Feminist: The Life of Alexandra Kollontai* [1979], p. 142). A similar misreading of international politics seems to have governed Stalin's behaviour in May–June 1941, when he discounted British warnings of imminent German attack as so much 'provocation': the British, as he saw it, obviously wanted to embroil Russia with Germany and then join Germany in a 'world-imperialist' onslaught on the workers' state. As British aid flowed in during the months of Russia's greatest need, the Soviet officials could conceal their delighted surprise only by complaining of the 'inadequacy' of this aid.
25. FO 371/3290/51340.
26. A. O. Chubaryan, *V. I. Lenin i formirovanie sovetskoi vneshnei politiki* (1972), p. 179.
27. A. O. Chubaryan, *Brestskii mir* (1964), pp. 157, 202. (Contrast the line of the British Communists, Mr and Mrs Coates, in their *Armed Intervention in Russia*, p. 74: 'There can be little doubt that had London and Washington acted on the sage advice tendered by Mr. Lockhart and Colonel Robins, Russia would not have quitted the war.') See also John M. Thompson's chapter in C. E. Black (ed.), *Rewriting Russian History* (1956), pp. 366–7.
28. Chubaryan, *V. I. Lenin*, p. 168. A. S. Bakhov, *Na zare sovetskoi diplomatii* (1966, p. 37) asserts that Trotsky's negotiations with Robins and Lockhart were carried on 'in secret from the Party and the Government'.
29. O. F. Solovyov, *Velikii Oktyabr i ego protivniki* (1968), p. 107. Cf. I. I. Mints, *God 1918-i* (1982): 'Lockhart hoped, with Trotsky's help, to organise intervention in the form of an "invitation" to the Anglo-American [*sic*] "Varangians" ' (p. 103).
30. W. Baumgart, 'Die Mission des Grafen Mirbach in Moskau, April–Juni 1918', in *Vierteljahrschift für Zeitgeschichte*, 16 (1968), pp. 85–6.
31. FO 371/3326/59429.
32. Sadoul, *Notes sur la Révolution bolchevique,* p. 304.
33. V. I. Petrov, *Otrazhenie stranoi sovetov nashestviya germanskogo imperializma v 1918 g.* (1980), p. 221, n. 364.
34. L. H. Grondijs, *La Guerre en Russie et en Sibérie* (1922), p. 272.
35. Niessel, *Le Triomphe des bolcheviks*, p. 288.
36. FO 371/3305/111409.

37. R. H. Ullman, *Anglo-Soviet Relations, 1917–1921*, vol. I, *Intervention and the War* (1961), p. 124.
38. *Bolshevik Propaganda*, pp. 810–11.
39. Richard K. Debo, *Revolution and Survival* (1979), p. 59.

5 THE GREAT GERMAN OFFENSIVE

1. *Labour Leader*, 24 January 1918, quoted in M. Fainsod, *International Socialism and the World War* (1935), pp. 172–3.
2. *Daily Herald*, 12 January 1918.
3. FO 371/3317/28147.
4. FO 371/3317/24390. Cf. Basil Thomson's memorandum of 21 February, alleging that Litvinov sought out soldiers of the British and American armies, in order to urge them to depose their officers and form soldiers' committees (FO 371/3299/37234).
5. *Dokumenty vneshnei politiki SSSR*, vol. I (1957), pp. 103–4.
6. FO 371/3315/29578.
7. CAB 24/43/3704.
8. FO 371/3323/46461. Cf. the reference in ch. 4 n. 10 above.
9. FO 371/3315/42956.
10. FO 371/3285/56926. Already on 16 February Lockhart had reported a conversation with Trotsky in which the latter undertook that 'if we will abandon our counter-revolutionary support in Russia, he will give quid pro quo as regards England' (FO 371/3299/31645).
11. FO 371/3299/70453. See also R. K. Debo, 'Litvinov and Kamenev – ambassadors extraordinary', in *Slavic Review*, September 1975, pp. 481–2.
12. Victor Serge, *Year One of the Russian Revolution* (1972), p. 312.
13. Middlebrook, *The Kaiser's Battle*, p. 339.
14. *Ursachen des Zusammenbruchs*, p. 225.
15. Quoted in H. R. Rudin, *Armistice 1918*, (1944), p. 3.
16. Ibid., p. 4.
17. Princess Evelyn Blücher, *An English Wife In Berlin* (1921), p. 211.
18. A. J. Toynbee, *History of the Peace Conference of Paris*, vol. I (1920), pp. 186–7.
19. H. W. Gatzke, *Germany's Drive to the West* (1966 edn), p. 260.
20. Serge, *Year One of the Russian Revolution*, p. 178.
21. Geoffrey Bruun, *Clemenceau* (1943), p. 155.
22. J. T. Wheeler-Bennett, *The Treaty of Brest-Litovsk and Germany's Eastern Policy* (1940), pp. 22–3.
23. C. A'C. Repington, *The First World War* (1920), vol. II, p. 331.
24. James Hinton, *The First Shop Stewards' Movement* (1973), p. 266.
25. The veracity of the Chilcott–Seely story was pooh-poohed in letters to me in 1983 by John Terraine (author of *To Win A War* [1978], and *Impacts of War* [1970] among other works on the Western Front in 1918); W. Moore (author of *The Thin Yellow Line* [1974]); and the Communist historian Andrew Rothstein (author of *The Soldiers' Strikes*

1919 [1980]). However, the subject of defeatism, in its widest sense, in Britain in 1918 should not be abandoned without mention of some sinister velleities in much higher places than the trenches of the Fifth Army. According to the *History of 'The Times'* (vol. 4, part 1 [1952], pp. 359–62), in April 1918

> the Prime Minister and ex-Ministers, including members of the War Cabinet and some members of the Labour Party, had privately discussed the possibility of ending the struggle in the West by giving the Germans a free hand in the East. It seemed an admirably complete and well-timed scheme, backed as it had been by the great Western German offensive of March and April. The Brest-Litovsk treaty offered, in the view of some, a perfect pretext for the Western Powers to appease Germany by sacrificing Russia.

When the story got about, there was vigorous counter-pressure. Wickham Steed wrote an editorial for the *Daily Mail* of 21 June strongly opposing any such move. British politicians who were toying with the idea that Germany might agree to evacuate Belgium and give up Alsace-Lorraine in return for a free hand in the East should realise that, if peace were to be made on this basis, Germany 'could, a few years hence, turn against the West with redoubled strength'. The article appeared 'four weeks before the British counter-offensive that was to change the whole situation. Nothing more was heard of the "free-hand" in Russia scheme.' (For Lord Milner's flirting with the idea of a separate peace with Germany at Russia's expense, see A. M. Gollin, *Proconsul in Politics* [1964], p. 523.)

6 SOVDEPIA UNDER GERMAN PRESSURE

1. In this study no attention is given to the German penetration of Georgia, important as this was for the German war effort (as a source of manganese), because that had no *direct* effect on the fortunes of the Bolshevik power in Petrograd and Moscow.
2. 'All we need now', wrote General Hoffmann on 4 April 1918, 'for the complete control of the Black Sea are the ports of Taganrog and Novorossiisk, and these we must have' (Hoffmann, *War Diaries and Other Papers*, vol. I, p. 213). Taganrog the Germans duly occupied, but not Novorossiisk. When Admiral Hopman urged that this port be occupied, he was informed (1 July) that troops could not be spared for this task (Baumgart (ed.), *Von Brest-Litovsk*, p. 536).
3. Regarding the German advances into Great Russia, in the directions of Bryansk, Kursk and Voronezh, Krassin wrote to his wife on 25 May, describing his conversations with German officials in Berlin: 'They cannot deny that, although Germany and Russia are nominally at peace, German troops are still advancing into our country. They simply say: "*Force majeure*; we have to plunder or go under" ' (Lubov Krassin, *Leonid Krassin* [1929], p. 82).

   The three points of the slogan with which the Bolsheviks came to power proved to be mutually contradictory. 'Peace, Bread, Land' –

yes, but 'peace' entailed, through German occupation of the Ukraine, loss of bread, and this, in turn, meant that, while the peasants got 'land', they had to surrender to requisitioning of the 'bread' it produced. Commenting on Lenin's speech of 14 January 1918, when he proposed the formation of armed detachments to go into the villages and extort grain from the peasants, Keep observes that the Bolshevik leader 'no doubt appreciated that the impending "annexationist peace" of Brest-Litovsk would deprive Soviet Russia of access to its most important source of food supplies and that drastic measures would be required to cope with the resultant shortages' (J. L. H. Keep, *The Russian Revolution* [1976], p. 425; Lenin, *Collected Works*, vol. 26, pp. 503–4, and vol. 42, pp. 52–3).

4. Ludendorff, *My War Memories* (1919), vol. II, p. 629; Chicherin, *Vneshnaya Politika Sov. Rossii za dva goda* (1920), p. 6.
5. Sadoul, *Notes sur la Révolution bolchevique*, p. 282.
6. Princess Blücher, *An English Wife in Berlin*, p. 200.
7. Lenin, *Collected Works*, vol. 27, pp. 330–1.
8. Ibid., vol. 27, p. 371.
9. Directive of 31 May, *Direktivy Glavnogo Komandovaniya Krasnoi Armii, 1917–20*, vol. I (1969), p. 46.
10. G. V. Chicherin, *Vneshnaya politika Sov. Rossii* (1920), p. 15.
11. Baumgart (ed.), *Von Brest-Litovsk*, p. 361.
12. Albert Norden, *Zwischen Berlin und Moskau* (1954), pp. 105–6, 129. Pamphlets appeared in Germany in the spring of 1918 which discussed how German capital would exploit the Trans-Siberian Railway and 'develop' Russian Turkestan (E. Tarle, *Evropa v epokhu imperializma*, p. 388).
13. *Dokumenty vneshnei politiki*, vol. I, p. 307. The arrangements for the exchange of prisoners-of-war reflected Germany's 'upper hand' in dealings with the Soviet Government and her determination to make the most of it. Instead of a mutual exchange of *all* prisoners, there was to be merely an exchange of equal numbers, 'head for head'. Germany thus retained a surplus of 1 200 000 Russians, whom she employed in her fields and factories, thereby freeing a similar number of Germans for service on the Western Front (Noulens, *Mon Ambassade en Russie sovietique*, [1933], vol. II, p. 93.)
14. V. L. Israelyan, 'Neopravdavshiisya prognoz grafa Mirbakha', in *Novaya i noveishaya istoriya*, no. 6 of 1967, p. 63.
15. Hoffmann, *War Diaries and Other Papers*, vol. I, p. 219. Looking back after the war, General Hoffmann recalled that 'in the spring of 1918 I supported the opinion that it would be best to clear the situation in the East – that is, to denounce the Peace, to march on Moscow, to form another Russian Government . . . and to conclude an alliance with the new Government' (ibid., vol. II, p. 228).
16. FO 371/3327/69398.
17. *Hansard*, 5th series, Commons, 1919, vol. 118, p. 1986. General Maynard records that 'during June, July and August no single unit was sent from east to west. For these three months the Murmansk force tied down the whole German army in Finland and put a stop to the transfer

to France of from three to four enemy divisions' (General G. C. M. Maynard, *The Murmansk Venture* [1928], p. 111).
18. M. Verstraete, *Mes Cahiers russes* (1920), p. 279.
19. Baumgart, 'Die Mission', p. 75.
20. Ludovic Naudeau, *En Prison sous la terreur russe* (1920), pp. 180–3.
21. Lenin, *Collected Works*, vol. 27, p. 355. On p. 380 Lenin summarises the content of the 'British ultimatum' here referred to as: 'If you cannot protect your neutrality, we shall wage war on your territory.'
22. Ibid., vol. 27, p. 361.
23. Debo, *Revolution and Survival*, pp. 219–20. This may be set against the claim made by Morgan Philips Price in *The Truth about the Allied Intervention in Russia* (1918) that, after Brest-Litovsk, the policy of the Soviet Government was 'a policy which aimed at maintaining the strictest neutrality between the two great fighting camps' (p. 10). Soviet neutrality in 1918 was somewhat like Soviet neutrality in 1940.
24. Many details of the heroic resistance in the Ukraine are given, from the archives, by V. I. Petrov, in his 1980 book mentioned in ch. 4 n. 33 above. See also the article by L. N. Zharova and I. I. Feldman on the defence of Kherson in the spring of 1918, in *Voprosy Istorii*, no. 1 of 1984.
25. This message is not included in Stalin's *Works*. See G. L. Nikol'nikov, *Vydayushchayasya pobeda leninskoy strategii i taktiki* (1968), p. 59; also D. V. Oznobishin, 'K istoriyu bor'by protiv "levykh kommunistov" posle VII s'ezda RKP(b)', in *Voprosy Istorii KPSS*, no. 10 of 1969, p. 35.
26. Nikol'nikov, op. cit., p. 74; A. A. Zaitsov, *1918 god* (1934), p. 82. It was to his participation in the fighting in the region on the borders of the Ukraine and the Don territory in this period that Khrushchev referred when he told Kennedy in October 1962: 'I have participated in two world wars' (R. Medvedev, *Khrushchev* [1982], p. 190).
27. Naida *et al.* (eds), *Istoriya grazhdanskoy voiny*, vol. 3, p. 138.
28. V. A. Antonov-Ovseyenko, *Zapiski o grazhdanskoy voine*, vol. II (1928), pp. 293–4.
29. I. K. Koblyakov, *Ot Bresta do Rapallo*, (1954), p. 33.
30. G. A. von Müller (ed. W. Görlitz), *The Kaiser and his Court* (1961), p. 355.
31. W. Baumgart, *Deutsche Ostpolitik 1918* (1966), p. 76.
32. V. M. Kholodkovskii, *Revolyutsiya 1918 goda v Finlandii i germanskaya interventsiya* (1967), p. 337.
33. Debo, 'Lockhart Plot or Dzerzhinsky Plot?', in *Journal of Modern History*, vol. XLIII, no. 3 (Sept. 1971), p. 423. (Cf. Lockhart, 27 and 28 May 1918, in FO 371/3286, pp. 66 and 126–7.)
34. O. Tokoi, *Sisu* (1957), pp. 173–4.
35. *Dokumenty vneshnei politiki*, vol. I, p. 313. Cf. ch. 4 n. 1 and 4, above. In his *Soviet History Atlas* (1979), Martin Gilbert has quite misunderstood the alignment of forces in North Russia. On p. 14 he states that the Allied troops there 'were joined by the Finnish troops under Mannerheim', and the arrows on his map showing White-Finnish moves towards Kem and Kandalaksha (his 'Kandalakskaya') are identical with

his 'Anglo-American' arrows. (And his map on p. 11 shows Archangel already under Allied occupation in March 1918!)

36. Quoted in Kennan, *The Decision to Intervene*, pp. 246–7.
37. T. Borenius, *Mannerheim* (1940), pp. 190–1.
38. FO 371/3307/84414.
39. W. E. Ironside, *Archangel 1918–1919* (1953), p. 17. A submarine base on the Kola Peninsula would have enabled the German Navy to outflank the mine-barrages that the Allies had laid across the North Sea. To oppose the Germans there was no British base nearer than the Orkneys.
40. Maynard, *The Murmansk Venture*, p. 110. The British Communist Andrew Rothstein utters not a word about the prospective submarine base in his book *When Britain Invaded Soviet Russia* (1979), devoted to the intervention in North Russia. Kholodkovskii, however, acknowledges that 'if the Germans were to emerge on the Murman Coast, that would mean a breach in the naval blockade to which Britain was subjecting Germany' – which does, at least, show awareness of the importance of that strip of seashore in relation to the Anglo-German conflict (*Revolyutsiya 1918*, p. 237). In the Second World War, during the period of the Nazi–Soviet Pact, the USSR granted facilities to the Germans in this same area for the establishment of a submarine base for operations against Britain. Only so late as 5 September 1940 did the German Foreign Office instruct their Ambassador in Moscow to inform the Soviets that the German Navy was giving up this base, because facilities were now available in occupied Norway. Schulenburg was instructed to thank the Soviet Government for their valuable assistance. The Ambassador replied on 9 September: 'Molotov expressed satisfaction that we had found useful the base placed at our disposal' (*Documents on German Foreign Policy*, Series D, vol. XI [1961], doct. no. 22).

    An article in *Voenno-istoricheskii zhurnal*, no. 5 of 1959, on German naval operations against the sea communications of Britain and the USA in the Second World War conspicuously fails to mention the submarine base on the Kola peninsula:

    > In the course of the war the system of bases was considerably extended as a result of the seizure by the German forces of ports and bases in Norway, Denmark, Holland, Belgium and France. . . . During the war the Germans secretly made use of ports in Spain, in Latin America and in other countries, (p. 35)

    (But perhaps the USSR comes under 'other countries'?)
41. *Dokumenty vneshnei politiki*, vol. I, p. 318: Kennan, *Decision to Intervene*, p. 269; J. Bunyan, *Intervention, Civil War and Communism in Russia, April–December 1918* (1936), p. 125.
42. *Leninskii Sbornik XI* (1931), p. 79. The fact that Stalin voted along with Sokolnikov is not mentioned in this publication, but is revealed in note 142 in vol. 27 of the 4th edition of Lenin's *Collected Works*. See also D. V. Oznobishin, *Ot Bresta do Yur'eva* (1966), p. 231.
43. L. I. Strakhovsky, *The Origins of American Intervention in Russia* (1937), pp. 105–6.

7 THE CZECHOSLOVAK REVOLT AND ITS CONSEQUENCES

1. Hoffmann, *War Diaries and Other Papers*, vol. II, p. 222: the emigré military historian A. A. Zaitsov says, in *1918 god*, p. 6, that 'the most serious resistance' encountered by the Germans in the Ukraine was at the hands of the Czechoslovaks, at Bakhmach, 7–10 March.
2. Quoted in W. H. Chamberlin, *The Russian Revolution* (1935), vol. II, p. 3.
3. V. A. Antonov-Ovseyenko, *Zapiski o grazhdanskoy voine*, vol. II, p. 94 and n. 2.
4. Victor M. Fic, *The Bolsheviks and the Czechoslovak Legion: The Origin of their Armed Conflict, March–May 1918* (1978), pp. 12–13. As Fic points out, subsequent Bolshevik claims that the movement of the Czechoslovak Legion was halted because of the landing of Japanese troops at Vladivostok do not hold water, since that landing did not take place until 5 April (p. 65, n. 12). In general, Fic finds flimsy Trotsky's argument about the danger of 'collusion' between the Japanese and the Czechoslovaks if the latter were allowed to reach the Far East.

   It was a lame argument to say that the presence of the Czechs in Vladivostok would increase the danger of intervention. In fact, the truth was just the reverse. Had the Allies really been contemplating to use these troops for launching their intervention, then the troops would have been ordered to hold fast to their strategic position in the proximity of the German front and in Central Russia, and not ordered to Vladivostok by the [Allied] Supreme War Council . . . (ibid., p. 245).

5. Ibid., p. 26; Bunyan, *Intervention*, p. 80.
6. J. F. N. Bradley, *Allied Intervention in Russia*, pp. 86–7 (see also his *The Civil War in Russia* [1975], p. 85); P. Golub, 'A glorious page of international solidarity', *Voenno-istoricheskii zhurnal*, no. 6 of 1965, pp. 94–5. This article mentions (p. 97) that those Czechoslovaks who did join the Red Army were quickly put to good use, participating in the suppression of a peasant revolt in Saratov province in early May.
7. Fic, *The Bolsheviks and the Czechoslovak Legion*, p. 29, quoting J. Kratochvil, *Cesta revoluce* (Prague, 1928), p. 63.
8. G. Bečvar, *The Lost Legion* (1939), p. 84.
9. From the history of the Sixth Regiment of the Czechoslovak Legion (*Za Svobodu*, Part III, p. 153), summarised for me by Sir Cecil Parrott in a letter of 1980.
10. Bunyan, *Intervention*, pp. 86–7; Bečvar, *The Lost Legion*, p. 91.
11. Bunyan, *Intervention*, p. 91; the original is Appendix no. 37 (p. 168) in V. Maksakov and A. Turunov, *Khronika grazhdanskoi voiny v Sibirii 1917–1918* (1926).
12. Bunyan, *Intervention*, pp. 93–4.
13. V. V. Garmiza, *Krushenie eserovskikh pravitel'stv* (1970), pp. 78–9.
14. FO 371/3324/107587.
15. Peter Fleming, *The Fate of Admiral Kolchak* (1963), p. 25.
16. E. A. Preobrazhenskii, *The Third Anniversary of the Russian October Revolution* (Glasgow, 1921), p. 10.

17. Baumgart, *Deutsche Ostpolitik 1918*, p. 218, n. 34: also Baumgart, 'Die Mission', pp. 86–90.
18. Ludendorff (ed.), *Urkunden der Obersten Heeresleitung über ihr Tätigkeit, 1916–1918* (1921), p. 490.
19. Baumgart (ed.), *Von Brest-Litovsk*, pp. 397–8.
20. Baumgart, 'Die Mission', p. 94.
21. FO 371/3286/115514.
22. Baumgart (ed.), *Von Brest-Litovsk*, p. 400. (*Oberost* was the HQ of the German forces in the Baltic provinces and north-western Russia.)
23. *Leninskii Sbornik*, XXXIV (1942), p. 25. As V. Lyakhov puts it, in a review of Sukhorukov's book on the XI Army in *Voenno-istoricheskii zhurnal*, no. 5 of 1962, the expedition against Taganrog 'was not co-ordinated with the general situation in the country created after the Brest peace' (p. 115).
24. V. T. Sukhorukov, *XI Armiya v boyakh na Severnom Kavkaze i Nizhnei Volge, 1918–1920 gg.* (1961), p. 36.
25. F. F. Raskolnikov, *Tales of Sub-Lieutenant Ilyin* (1982), pp. 37, 42–3, 53); I. Borisenko, *Sov. respubliki na Severnom Kavkaze v 1918 godu* (1930), p. 171 seq.). When the Germans entered Sevastopol, the ships of Russia's Black Sea Fleet left that port and sailed to Novorossiisk. The Germans demanded that the ships return to Sevastopol. Chicherin suggested a compromise, whereby the ships remain at Novorossiisk, but be placed under German supervision, 'so as to leave no doubt of their harmlessness to the German naval forces' (*Dokumenty vneshnei politiki SSSR*, vol. I, pp. 330–1). But the Germans were obdurate. Accordingly, the Moscow Government sent two sets of instructions to Novorossiisk – one, in clear, for the ships to be handed over to the Germans, the other, in cipher, for them to be scuttled. Many of the sailors concerned were, naturally, unhappy about scuttling their ships, and some were Ukranian patriots or Left SRs who wanted to fight the Germans.

    There was also very strong feeling among the Bolsheviks in the Kuban–Black Sea Republic against either returning the ships to Sevastopol or scuttling them, and having been warned by Moscow that they were endangering the survival of the RSFSR, they briefly separated their republic from the federation and then 'called on the sailors to fight to the last shell' (A. I. Kozlov, 'Chernomorskii flot i sov.–germanskie otnosheniya v 1918 godu', in *Voenno-istoricheskii zhurnal*, no. 5 of 1984, p. 42. This article makes it clear that Lenin's chief concern was to stop the 'Left' element from using the ships against the Germans.) N. Monasterev, in *Dans la Mer Noire* (1928), says that only a minority of the officers favoured scuttling, and that some considered that, as it was already clear to them that the Germans had lost the war, it would make no difference if the ships were returned to Sevastopol (p. 190).

    F. F. Raskolnikov was sent by Lenin to Novorossiisk to implement the Government's policy, and, after some of the ships had sailed back to Sevastopol, succeeded in having the remainder scuttled before the expiry of the German ultimatum on 18 June.

    Arkhiv Russkoy Revolyutsii, vol. 14 (1924), includes a remarkable collection of documents relating to the struggle over the Black Sea

Fleet between March and June 1918, which reveal the embarrassment caused to the Moscow Government by the 'uncontrollable' elements in the fleet.

26. Lubov Krassin, *Leonid Krassin*, pp. 90–9.
27. CAB 24/145, p. 61.
28. FO 371/3305/111415; FO 371/3286/120496.
29. *Dokumenty vneshnei politiki*, vol. I, p. 375. Lenin told Chicherin on 27 June that the German Embassy had informed him that, although the Germans did not want to have to invade Soviet Russia, they expected the Bolsheviks to act firmly against the British at Murmansk, who had strengthened their expeditionary force: Chicherin must send a sharp note to the British at once. This was duly done. It proved the last straw for the Murmansk Soviet, which decided not to obey any more orders from Moscow. (Tokoi and his force of Red Finns who had been fighting alongside the British also now finally broke with Moscow.) There was a piquant exchange on the direct wire on 2 July, between Trotsky and Yuriev, the chairman of the Murmansk Soviet. *Trotsky*: 'I presume General Poole stands behind you and dictates your statements.' *Yuriev*: 'And I presume that Count Mirbach stands behind you and dictates your statements.' (*Leninskii Sbornik*, XXXVII [1970], pp. 90–1; C. Jay Smith, *Finland and the Russian Revolution 1917–22* [1958], pp. 110–11; L. I. Strakhovsky, *The Origins of American Intervention in North Russia* [1931], p. 68.)
30. Karl von Bothmer, *Mit Graf Mirbach in Moskau* (1922), pp. 63–4; Baumgart, *Deutsche Ostpolitik 1918*, p. 345. Lockhart telegraphed on 21 June that Chicherin and Karakhan were 'amused at the idea that they had accepted German help for the purpose of crushing' the Czechoslovaks (CAB 24/145, p. 58).
31. Admiral Hopman's diary, 1 July, in Baumgart (ed.), *Von Brest-Litovsk*, p. 536.
32. FO 371/3327/110747.
33. Baumgart (ed.), *Von Brest-Litovsk*, p. 401. 'The German divisions on the Eastern Front, bled white by the renewal of all their combat-capable elements, became less and less fit to carry out the plans for armed struggle against the Bolsheviks which the German High Command undoubtedly entertained' (A. A. Zaitsov, *1918 god*, p. 112).
34. N. N. Golovin, *Rossiiskaya kontr-revolyutsiya v 1917–1918 gg.* (1937), Part III, p. 91. The Germans became nervous even regarding their good friend the Don Ataman, P. N. Krasnov, and sent a special mission to Novocherkassk to obtain from him a clear statement as to his attitude towards the Czechoslovaks. Krasnov promised to observe 'neutrality' (A. A. Zaitsov, *1918 god*, pp. 156–7).
35. D. Lehovich, *White Against Red: The Life of General Anton Denikin* (1974), pp. 221–3, 250; P. M. Volkonskii, *The Volunteer Army of Alexeiev and Denikin: a short historical sketch of the army from its origin to November 1/14, 1918* (1919), p. 25.
36. *Dokumenty vneshnei politiki*, vol. I, p. 378.
37. A. I. Denikin, *Ocherki russkoi smuty*, vol. III (1924), p. 116.
38. CAB 24/145, p. 61.

39. V. Zhuravlev, *Dekrety sov. vlasti kak istorichesky istochnik* (1979), pp. 268–9; S. Liberman, *Building Lenin's Russia* (1945), pp. 24–5.
40. V. I. Petrov, *Otrazhenie stranoi sovetov*, p. 241.
41. S. Dernberg *et al.* (eds), *Sovetski-germanskie otnosheniya ot peregovorov v Brest-Litovske do podpisaniya Rapallskogo dogovora*, vol. I (1968), p. 573.
42. H. W. Gatzke, 'Zu den deutsch-russichen Beziehungen im Sommer 1918', in *Vierteljahrshefte für Zeitgeschichte*, 3 (1955), pp. 86–7, 91.
43. *Sovetsko–germanskie otnosheniya*, vol. I, pp. xvi, 576: Baumgart, *Deutsche Ostpolitik 1918*, p. 87.

8 THE MIRBACH CRISIS

1. Murmansk is actually spelt 'Mourmansk' in the title and in the text. A copy of this broadsheet is in the British Library of Political and Economic Science at the LSE, catalogued as R (S.R.) 1109. P217918. The allusion in this document to 'the same crowd that betrayed Kitchener' refers to the legends then circulating about the death at sea of Field-Marshal Lord Kitchener, in 1916. The Russian Government had invited him to come over and help improve the organisation of Russia's war effort. His ship was sunk by a German mine, off the Orkneys. Some said that 'the pro-German clique around the Tsaritsa' had betrayed him; others, such as Ludendorff, fingered 'the Jews and Freemasons'.
2. See also the references to it in A. S. Yakushevskii, *Propagandistskaya rabota bolshevikov sredi voisk interventov v 1918–20 gg.* (1974), pp. 68, 137. The relative suddenness of the change of attitude by the Bolsheviks is reflected in two despatches from General Poole, at Murmansk, to the War Office. On 2 June he reported on a visit by Moscow's emissary Natsarenus: 'We parted on excellent terms and with a mutual understanding of unofficial co-operation. I think he is pleased to have our help and will back us as far as possible' (WO 33/962 [no. 7]). On 30 June he had to report that Natsarenus was approaching with troops to fight the British, and the garrison at Kandalaksha was being reinforced in order to stop him (WO 33/962 [no. 30]).
3. FO 371/3335/151078.
4. V. I. Mashezerskii, *Pobeda velikogo oktyabrya i obrazovanie sovetskoy avtonomii Karelii* (1978), p. 54.
5. A. Paquet, *Im kommunistischen Russland* (1919), p. 28.
6. *Dokumenty vneshnei politiki*, vol. I, p. 360. Cf. G. A. Solomon, *Sredi krasnykh vozhdei* (1930), vol. I, pp. 80–3.
7. *Biografischeskaya Khronika V. I. Lenina*, vol. 5 (1974), p. 631. Gustav Hilger, who was in the German Embassy at the time, expressed the view that the Bolsheviks sensed 'that Germany was no longer strong enough to insist on the fulfilment of her demands' (G. Hilger and A. G. Meyer, *The Incompatible Allies* [1953], p. 9).
8. FO 371/3287/130470. Helfferich was told in Berlin before his departure for Moscow to replace Mirbach, on 24 July, 'that Germany had no

forces to spare for Russian adventures' (J. G. Williamson, *Karl Helfferich, 1872–1924* [1971], p. 275). Cf. the admission in the diary of a German embassy official, on 27 July, that owing to developments on the Western Front, the day was 'well behind us' when the Germans could do as they liked in the East (Von Bothmer, *Mit Graf Mirbach in Moskau*, p. 112).

A few days after the murder of his ambassador in Moscow, the Kaiser acknowledged the sad fact that, 'right now, we have to support the Bolsheviks under any circumstances' (G. Freund, *Unholy Alliance* [1957], p. 22). Colonel A. Bauermeister, a German military intelligence officer, tells, in *Spies Break Through* (1934), how he was approached in Reval by a girl who offered to shoot Lenin. He replied: 'If Lenin were to be murdered, the Bolsheviks might possibly fall. But in their place would come a government which would declare war against Germany. You will therefore see that, however much we may detest him and his fellows, we are not concerned to have Lenin murdered' (pp. 164–6).

9. Arthur Ransome, *Autobiography* (1976), pp. 244–5.
10. A. F. Ilyin-Zhenevskii, *The Bolsheviks in Power: Reminiscences of the Year 1918* (English translation, 1984) p. 114. Some historians doubt the veracity of the official Soviet story about the murder of Mirbach, and consider that, if the Bolsheviks did not directly inspire the murder, they at least deliberately allowed it to take place, in order to have an excuse to crush the Left SRs, who were dangerous opponents of Bolshevik policy towards the peasants. For a recent summary of the evidence, see Yu. G. Fel'shtinskii, *Bolsheviki i levye eseri okt. 1917–iyul 1918* (1985). Fel'shtinskii thinks (p. 263) that Lenin understood, 'no worse than Steinberg', that in July 1918 Germany was no longer in a position to attack Soviet Russia.
11. Baumgart, *Deutsche Ostpolitik 1918*, pp. 240–1.
12. Lenin, *Collected Works*, vol. 44, pp. 114–15.
13. Ibid., vol. 27, 533.

9 FACTORS IN GERMANY'S FAILURE IN THE WEST

1. J. L. Stokesbury, *A Short History of the First World War* (1981), p. 270.
2. C. N. Barclay, *Armistice 1918*, p. 14.
3. Gough, *The March Retreat*, p. 181.
4. Madelin, *La Bataille de France*, p. 111.
5. J. Terraine, *The Smoke and the Fire: Myths and Anti-Myths of War, 1861–1945* (1980), p. 156.
6. Quoted in R. H. Lutz, *The Causes of the German Collapse in 1918* (1934), p. 146.
7. M. Beer, *Fifty Years of International Socialism* (1935), p. 178.
8. Farrer-Hockley, *Goughie*, p. 307.
9. Jünger, *Storm of Steel*, pp. 267–8. Cf. Correlli Barnett, *The Swordbearers* (1963), p. 317, and H. Sulzbach, *With The German Guns* (1973), p. 157.

10. Ludendorff, *My War Memories* (1919), p. 611.
11. Von Müller, *The Kaiser and his Court*, p. 349.
12. Rudolf Binding, *A Fatalist at War* (1929), pp. 209–11, 218.
13. C. R. M. F. Cruttwell, *History of the Great War, 1914–18* (1934), p. 519.
14. J. F. C. Fuller, *Decisive Battles, Their Influence upon History*, vol. II (1940), p. 296.
15. Cruttwell, *History of the Great War*, p. 530.
16. Jünger, *Storm of Steel*, p. 289.
17. M. Saunders and P. M. Taylor, *British Propaganda during the First World War* (1982), p. 220.
18. F. I. Notovich, 'Razgrom chetvertogo soyuza v 1918 godu', in *Istoricheskii zhurnal*, no. 7–8 of 1941, p. 49.
19. Ludendorff, *My War Memories*, p. 679.
20. *The Private Papers of Douglas Haig, 1914–1919* (1952), p. 324. Smuts, at the Imperial War Cabinet of 14 August, said: 'We may reach the end of 1919 with the West still an indecisive theatre' (CAB 23/43, p. 8).
21. *Direktivy*, p. 103.
22. *Biograficheskaya Khronika*, vol. 5, 667.
23. Ibid., vol. 5, p. 670, and vol. 6, p. 16.
24. T. J. Uldricks, *Diplomacy and Ideology* (1979), p. 39, echoing Wheeler-Bennett; cf. Louis Fischer, *The Soviets in World Affairs* (1930), vol. I, p. 130: 'Joffe misinformed Moscow on the strength of the Central Powers. He did not expect that their collapse was so imminent.'
25. Baumgart, *Deutsche Ostpolitik*, pp. 256–7. Our knowledge of this period is restricted by the circumstances that the minutes of meetings of the Central Committee of the Soviet Communist Party between 19 May and 16 September, 1918, 'have not yet been found' (V. V. Anikeev, *Deyatelnost Ts K RSDRP (b) v 1917–1918 gg. Khronika sobytii* [1974], p. 298, n.)

10 THE TRAGEDY OF BAKU

1. CAB 27/26: E. C. 263.
2. R. MacDonell, '. . . *And Nothing Long*' (1938), pp. 212–13.
3. WO 95/5043 (Dunsterforce War Diary Appendixes, Ops General, February–May 1918), p. 96a.
4. Ibid., p. 97a.
5. Nikol'nikov, *Vydayushchayasya pobeda leninskoy strategii i taktiki*, p. 257.
6. Lenin, *Collected Works*, vol. 44, p. 111.
7. *Krasnyi Archiv*, vol. 45 (89–90) (1938), p. 19.
8. Ibid., p. 20.
9. Mints, *God 1918-i*, p. 471.
10. *Leninskii Sbornik*, 38 (1975), p. 212.
11. *Dokumenty*, pp. 401–2.
12. Lenin, *Collected Works*, vol. 35, p. 342.

13. L. M. Lifshits, *Geroicheskii podvig bakinskikh bolshevikov* (1964), p. 230.
14. *Dokumenty*, p. 412.
15. Lenin, *Collected Works*, vol. 35, p. 345.
16. Ibid., vol. 28, pp. 21–4.
17. Ibid., vol. 35, p. 348.
18. Ibid., vol. 35, p. 608, note 329.
19. *Dokumenty*, p. 423.
20. CAB 27/31: E. C. 1215.
21. For a critical analysis of another Soviet myth, concerning 'the 26 Baku Commissars', see the contributions by Brian Pearce to *Sbornik* (the annual bulletin of the Study Group on the Russian Revolution), nos. 6–7 (1981), 9 (1983) and 11 (1985).
22. G. V. Chicherin, *Vneshnaya politika sovetskoi Rossii za dva goda* (1920), p. 20; W. Baumgart, 'Die "geschäftliche Behandlung" des Berliner Ergänzerungsvertrag vom 27 August 1918', in *Historisches Jahrbuch*, 89 (1969), pp. 146–8; R. Hovannisian, *Armenia on the Road to Independence* (1967), p. 223.
23. One gets an impression from the documents that a certain amount of the Central Soviet Government's aid intended for Baku proceeded no further than Tsaritsyn, where Stalin intercepted it for use in the defence of that key centre. It may be that he decided that Baku was indefensible and anything sent there would merely be expended to no purpose, whereas at Tsaritsyn it could help in a vital task. A. V. Antonov-Ovseyenko, the civil-war commander's son, in *The Time of Stalin: Portrait of a Tyranny* (1981), alleges that Shaumyan was convinced that he would get no help from Stalin (p. 10). Tsaritsyn seems to have been a bottleneck also for aid from the centre to the isolated Bolshevik stronghold in Central Asia: Lenin informed Kolesov (in Tashkent) on 23 August: 'As regards the military aid [which had been promised him], we do not know where it is. We think it is held up near Tsaritsyn' (Lenin, *Collected Works*, vol. 44, pp. 140–1).

    V. T. Sukhorukov, in *XI Armiya v boyakh na Severnom Kavkaze i Nizhnei Volge, 1918–1920 gg.* (1961), considers that Stalin underestimated the importance of the struggle going on in Caucasia: 'Only thus is it possible to understand J. V. Stalin's order in August [1918] for the despatch from Astrakhan to Tsaritsyn of 15 million cartridges which had been destined mainly for Baku and North Caucasia' (p. 76). The authors (Naida and Naumov) of Chapter 4 in the symposium edited by P. A. Zhilin, *Ocherki po istoriografii sovetskogo obshchestva* (1965), regret that Stalin 'did not show proper initiative and skill in the matter of giving aid to the North-Caucasia army and the forces fighting in Baku' (p. 181). A glimpse of some of the difficulties involved is given by V. Solomennyi in his article on the 'First Lenin Revolutionary Regiment', in *Voenno-istoricheskii zhurnal*, no. 4 of 1962. This regiment had been raised in the Chernigov and Gomel areas, and when ordered to proceed to Baku was unwilling to move from its home ground, where fighting was still going on. Starting out, eventually, on 3 August, owing to various obstacles and delays they did not reach

Astrakhan until 14–15 August – and then were required to stay there in order to suppress a local revolt (p. 111).

Though only 'a sideshow of a sideshow', the campaign of Dunsterforce was a notable feat of arms. 'We had no cause to reproach ourselves. . . . Playing a lone hand, let down by all who should have helped us, fighting alongside troops who, we knew, were utterly unreliable, hemmed in by intrigue more dangerous than enemy attacks, we kept at bay for a period of six weeks almost ten times our numbers' (Anon., 'Further adventures of the armoured cars: Persia and Baku', in *Blackwood's Magazine*, March 1919). Roy Maclaren, the historian of *Canadians in Russia, 1918–19* (1976), points out that,

> if German resistance had not collapsed in the summer of 1918, if the war had dragged on into 1919, as some thought it would, no doubt the little campaign of Dunsterforce would now be recalled in the annals of the Allied forces as a minor but useful enterprise that delayed the Central Powers in their attempt to exploit the resources of southern Russia. (p. 35)

The American historian Louis Fischer claimed in his *The Soviets in World Affairs*, vol. I (1930), p. 87, that Dunsterforce left Baku 'without firing a shot'. (The same writer manages to gloss over the significance for Russia of the Allied victory in France by these phrases: 'Fortunately for Russia . . ., the Brest-Litovsk terms had no permanent influence on European geography. The boundaries it outlined were soon erased. But the peace would have been extremely expensive . . . had matters developed differently. . . . However, as it happened, the practical results of Brest were of short duration' [ibid., p. 68].)

In view of the Bolsheviks' firm stand in August 1918 against accepting any British aid, it is interesting to read Stalin's appeal to Churchill on 13 September 1941 to 'land 25–30 divisions at Archangel or ship them to the southern areas of the USSR via Iran for military co-operation with the Soviet troops on Soviet soil . . .' (*Stalin's Correspondence with Churchill, Attlee, Roosevelt and Truman, 1941–45* [Moscow, 1957], vol. I, p. 24). But that, of course, was after a period of collaboration with Germany had been ended, catastrophically, on the Germans' initiative – a turn of events which, though threatened, did not come about in 1918.

11 'PARALLEL ACTION'

1. Baumgart (ed.), *Von Brest-Litovsk*, p. 81.
2. S. Zarnitskii and A. Sergeyev, *Chicherin* (2nd edn, 1975), p. 114.
3. The 'address' was published in *Izvestiya* and *Pravda*, and is reprinted in *Dekrety sovetskoi vlasti*, vol. III (1964), p. 128. An English translation is given in Bunyan, *Intervention*, p. 142. On 8 August Lenin signed an appeal to Russian citizens in France not to join the French Army or Foreign Legion (*Dekrety*, pp. 191–2).
4. K. Helfferich, *Der Weltkrieg*, vol. III (1919), pp. 466–7. This Soviet proposal for German intervention has become a sort of dirty secret in

Soviet historiography. Although Chicherin wrote about it frankly in an article in *Izvestiya* of 30 January 1924 which was reproduced ('Lenin i vneshnaya politika') in *Mirovaya politika v 1924 g.* (1924), the passage dealing with it was omitted when this article was reprinted in *Vospominanya o V. I. Lenine*, vol. III [1969], p. 485 seq., and in Chicherin's *Stati i rechi* (1961). In his 'Letter to American Workers' dated 20 August 1918 Lenin referred to the alliance made between the American fighters for independence and the French and Spanish enemies of Britain, and said that he would not hesitate, if necessary, 'to enter into a similar "agreement"' with the Germans as the one he had made with the French military mission in February 1918. The 'explanatory notes' to the *Collected Works* say nothing about the negotiations with the Germans already undertaken at that time (Lenin, *Collected Works*, vol. 28, pp. 67–8). However, the German Communist historian G. Rosenfeld writes without inhibition on this matter, quoting from Chicherin's original 1924 article (*Sowjetrussland und Deutschland, 1917–22* [1960], p. 120). Gromyko and Ponomarev, in their book on Soviet foreign policy, write blandly: 'The Soviet Government pursued an independent policy of strict neutrality and did not assist the Germans in their fight against the Entente . . .' (*History of Soviet Foreign Policy*, vol. I, p. 87).

5. Baumgart (ed.), *Von Brest-Litvosk*, p. 94.
6. Ritter, *The Sword and the Sceptre*, vol. IV (1973), p. 263.
7. Ibid., p. 276; H. Herwig, 'German Policy in the Eastern Baltic Sea in 1918', *Slavic Review*, June 1973, p. 348. A Soviet historian writes of this period: 'Study of the documents enables us to conclude that in June–July 1918 a section of the ruling upper circles of Germany, in particular the military and the political groups close to them, had a burning desire to go over to open support of the counter-revolutionary forces in Russia, with a view to overthrowing Soviet power and restoring the monarchy' (A. A. Akhtamzyan, in V. A. Maslennikov (ed.), *Iz istorii agressivnoi vneshnei politiki germanskogo imperializma* (1959), p. 119.
8. *Baltiiskie moryaki v bor'be za vlast' sovetov (noyabr' 1917–dekabr' 1918)*, vol. II (1968), pp. 212–13: Baumgart, 'Unternehmen "Schlussstein"', in *Wehrwissenschaftliche Rundschau*, 19 (1969), pp. 345–8.
9. E. H. Carr, *The Bolshevik Revolution*, vol. I (1950), p. 83.
10. Baumgart, 'Unternehmen "Schlussstein"', p. 334.
11. Ibid., p. 335.
12. Ibid., p. 470; Baumgart, *Deutsche Ostpolitik 1918*, pp. 114–15.
13. Baumgart, 'Unternehmen "Schlussstein"', pp. 354–5; Baumgart, *Deutsche Ostpolitik 1918*, p. 116.
14. R. Von der Goltz, *Meine Sendung in Finnland und im Baltikum* (1920), p. 92. (Repeated in the re-edition of 1936, entitled *Als politischer General im Osten*, p. 62).
15. Gatzke, 'Zu den deutsch-russischen Beziehungen', p. 93.
16. Ibid., p. 94.
17. Baumgart, *Deutsche Ostpolitik 1918*, pp. 248–9.

18. Ritter, *The Sword and the Sceptre*, p. 264.
19. I. K. Koblyakov, 'Bor'ba sov. gosudarstva za sokhranenie mira s Germanie v periode deistviya Brestskogo dogovora', in *Istoriya SSSR*, no. 4 of 1958, p. 20.
20. In this 1924 article on Lenin and Soviet foreign policy Chicherin mentioned that it was in the summer of 1918, in relation to Germany, that Lenin first gave concrete form to his plans for attracting foreign capital and making large-scale concessions available to it (Chicherin, *Stati i rechi* [1961], p. 279).
21. *Canadian–American Slavic Studies*, no. 4 of 1974, p. 562.
22. Baumgart (ed.), *Von Brest-Litovsk*, p. 114.
23. Lenin, *Collected Works*, vol. 28, p. 86; he was addressing the First All-Russia Congress on Education. Five days earlier, he had rejoined that, according to evidence at the Malvy trial, 'thousands of [French] soldiers have refused to go to the front' (ibid., p. 82). And Chicherin had told Paquet on 22 August that Britain was on the brink of 'a revolutionary movement' (*Von Brest-Litovsk*, p. 121).
24. *The Call* (London), 5 September 1918.
25. Debo, *Revolution and Survival*, p. 341; Baumgart, *Deutsche Ostpolitik 1918*, p. 110.
26. Lenin, *Collected Works*, vol. 44, p. 128.
27. *Sovetskie Arkhivy*, 1980 (2), pp. 12, 13, 15; V. I. Yegoryev (Commander of the Western Sector), in A. Bubnov, S. Kamenev and R. Eideman (eds), *Grazhdanskaya voina 1918–1921 gg.*, vol. I (1928), p. 244.
28. Trotsky, *On Lenin*, p. 133.
29. V. I. Petrov, *Otrazhenie*, p. 246; cf. S. V. Lipitskii, *Leninskoye rukovodstvo oboronoi strany* (1979), p. 98.
30. Article on the Supreme War Council in Khromov's encyclopaedia of the civil war, op. cit., p. 138.
31. Debo, *Revolution and Survival*, p. 342.
32. Baumgart, 'Unternehmen "Schlussstein" ', pp. 462–4. When the attempt on Lenin's life raised the danger that the Soviet Government might fall, 'Operation "Capstone"' was (4 September) momentarily reactivated, *Oberost* being ordered to get ready to march on Petrograd. (ibid., p. 353).
33. Baumgart, *Deutsche Ostpolitik 1918*, pp. 315–17.

12 THE SUPPLEMENTARY TREATY

1. Rosenfeld, *Sowjetrussland und Deutschland 1917–22* (1960), p. 123.
2. Akhtamzyan, in Maslennikov, *Iz istorii agressivnoi vneshnoi politiki germanskogo imperializma*, p. 129.
3. Gatzke, *Germany's Drive*, pp. 177–9.
4. The text of the treaty is in *Dokumenty*, pp. 437–45. This Soviet publication does not, of course, give the secret protocol attached to it. An English translation of both the public and the secret parts of the

treaty is given as Appendices VII and VIII to J. T. Wheeler-Bennett, *Brest-Litovsk: The Forgotten Peace* (1938).
5. Smith, *Finland and the Russian Revolution, 1917–22*, p. 117.
6. FO 371/3308/155934; P. Renouvin, *War and Aftermath, 1914–1929* (1968), p. 98.
7. Ritter, *The Sword and the Sceptre*, p. 286.
8. Wheeler-Bennett, *Brest-Litovsk*, pp. 344–5.
9. Akhtamzyan, in Maslennikov, op. cit., p. 132. A Dutch politician remarked, concerning the indemnity extorted from Russia: 'The Germans still go on robbing even on their death-bed' (M. Erzberger, *Souvenirs de Guerre* [1921], p. 364).
10. Carr, *The Bolshevik Revolution*, p. 85. The secret part of the treaty was published, from the German archives, in *Europäische Gespräche*, 4 (1926), pp. 148–53. 'This, probably, was the first secret agreement of Lenin, who a short time before had made public the secret agreements of the old Russian Government and who rejected in principle every form of secret diplomacy' (D. Dallin, *Russian and Postwar Europe* [1945], p. 69).
11. Gatzke, 'Zu den deutsch-russichen Beziehungen', p. 77.
12. *Pravda*, 7 September 1918, quoted in Baumgart, *Deutsche Ostpolitik*, p. 310, n. 180.
13. Ulam, *Expansion and Coexistence*, p. 89.
14. Baumgart, *Deutsche Ostpolitik*, p. 301.
15. I. M. Maiskii, *Vneshnaya politika RSFSR, 1917–22* (1922), pp. 46–7.
16. L. Fischer, *The Soviets in World Affairs* (1930), vol. I, p. 130, n. 2. Similar observations are made by Carr, G. Freund and others. Wheeler-Bennett (*Brest-Litovsk*, p. 347) does observe that 'the explanation lies, in all probability, in the internal situation of Russia . . .'.
17. Baumgart, *Deutsche Ostpolitik*, pp. 316–17.
18. Baumgart, *Von Brest-Litovsk*, p. 163.
19. Although considerable unpleasantness marked their first contacts. Novorossiisk was dominated by the guns of German warships, and when the famous Taman Army was passing through the town on its way southward, hotly pursued by White Cossacks, these warships 'opened strong artillery fire, first on the Whites, who were coming down from the hills and then on our third column. . . . The Germans then renewed their firing on the Whites. Soon there was a vigorous exchange of fire between the Germans and the Cossacks. While they were fighting each other, our units succeeded in leaving the town in good order.' (E. Kovtyukh, *'Zheleznyi potok' v voennom izlozhenii* [3rd edn, 1935], p. 39).

    Sukhorukov, in his article on the campaign of the Taman Army in *Sovetskaya Istoricheskaya Entsiklopediya*, vol. XIV, says nothing about the Germans firing on the Red troops. According to V. P. Gorlov (*Geroicheskii pokhod* [1963], p. 35) Novorossiisk 'was regarded as neutral, but was essentially in the hands of the German and Turkish interventionists', by which he evidently means that the warships offshore could control the town's fate. It was full of 'Red' sailors from the scuttled ships of the Black Sea Fleet, and as the threat from the

Volunteer Army grew, the Kuban Soviets asked the Germans, in vain, formally to occupy the town (Admiral Hopman, diary entry of 25 August 1918, in Baumgart (ed.), *Von Brest-Litovsk*, p. 575).
20. Ibid., pp. 578, 585, 586, 593.
21. P. Kenez, *Civil War in South Russia, 1918* (1971), p. 246.
22. Volkonskii, *The Volunteer Army*, p. 29.
23. Denikin, *Ocherki russkoi smuty*, vol. 3, p. 239.
24. Solomon, *Sredi krasnykh vozhdei*, vol. I, pp. 101–5, 115n.; see also I. K. Koblyakov, 'Bor'ba sov. gosudarstva za sokhranenie mira s Germaniei v perioda deistviya Brestkogo dogovora', in *Istoria SSSR*, no. 4 of 1958, p. 15.
25. Hoffmann, *War Diaries and Other Papers*, vol. I, p. 235.
26. Ludendorff, *My War Memories*, p. 699: Akhtamzyan, in Maslennikov, op. cit., p. 135.
27. Baumgart, *Deutsche Ostpolitik*, p. 330, n. 104. Radek wrote, years later, that the news that Germany had asked for an armistice was, for the Bolsheviks,

> like the news of liberation. The situation had much deteriorated in the last months. Our intelligence reports showed that the ring round the neck of Soviet Russia was tightening from day to day . . . White detachments were training in Pskov. Rakovsky, passing through Vienna, saw in a hotel a completely undisguised signboard of a recruiting office. . . . In our opinion the Germans were reckoning with the return of Belgium to the Allies and were therefore preparing to seize Moscow and Petrograd, in order to have in their hands a bargaining counter. . . . But now the Germans were offering talks on peace. Obviously the position at the front was worse than we had assumed (article in *Krasnaya Nov*, October 1926, translated in E. H. Carr, 'Radek's "Political Salon" in Berlin, 1919', *Soviet Studies*, April 1952).

28. Lenin, *Collected Works*, vol. 28, p. 122.

13 THE END IN THE WEST

1. Jünger, *Storm of Steel*, pp. 303–4.
2. FO 371/3309/114240.
3. *Ursachen*, p. 159.
4. Nikol'nikov, *Vydayuschayasya pobeda leninskoi strategii i taktiki*, p. 275.
5. Ludendorff, *My War Memories*, p. 642.
6. Ritter, *The Sword and the Sceptre*, vol. 4, p. 232.
7. R. H. Lutz, *The Causes of the German Collapse in 1918* (1934), p. 166.
8. Hoffmann, *War Diaries and Other Papers*, vol. 2, p. 231.
9. A. J. Berlau, *The German Social-Democratic Party, 1914–21* (1949), p. 171.
10. Wheeler-Bennett, *Brest-Litovsk*, pp. 353–4.
11. Tarle, *Evropa v epokhu imperializma*, pp. 437–8.

12. Lenin, *Collected Works*, vol. 28, p. 133.
13. Cf. Rosenberg, in *Ursachen*, pp. 105–10. On 12 November 1918 the new German Government confirmed the retention of officers' powers of command, stressing the importance of ensuring orderly withdrawal of the army into Germany within the fifteen days allowed by the Armistice. Karl Liebknecht denounced this 'counter-revolutionary' policy. 'That few of the soldiers would have agreed with Liebknecht is evident from the attitude of the soldiers' council at GHQ when Groener explained to them the organisational complexities involved. The councils in the field army indeed showed little desire to go beyond the welfare function assigned to them.' (A. J. Ryder, *The German Revolution*, p. 161). The main role played by German soldiers (as against sailors) in the stormy politics of 1918–20 was as anti-Communist *Freikorpskämpfer*.
14. K. Spalding and K. Brooke, *Historical Dictionary of German Figurative Usage*, vol. II (1967), under 'Dolchstoss'; *Meyers Neues Lexikon* (Leipzig), vol. 3 (1972), under 'Dolchstosslegende'; John Terraine, letter to me, 25 February 1983. M. E. Occleshaw, 'The "Stab in the Back" – Myth of Reality?' (*RUSI*, September 1985) strives to show that the relation between Allied subversive activity in Germany and the effect of Germany's military defeat was 'a two-way traffic', but is unable convincingly to conceal the priority of military defeat as the cause of Germany's collapse. He jumps over the period between March and July 1918, and then observes that, 'by the late summer of 1918 the fact that they had lost the war was apparent to many Germans'! His article is valuable, though, in demonstrating the importance of Allied, as against Bolshevik, propaganda in Germany.
15. Yet, later in the same work, Trotsky claimed: 'By our international policy we not only did not assist the Hohenzollern to assume a position of world domination; on the contrary, by our November Revolution we did more than anyone else to prepare his overthrow' (ibid., p. 124); and in 1939 he wrote: 'Hohenzollern militarism was overthrown completely by the October Revolution' ('A Step Towards Social-Patriotism', 7 March 1939, in *Writings of Leon Trotsky 1938–39* [1974], p. 213).

14 CONCLUSION

1. Trotsky, *The War and the International*, reprinted in 1918 as *The Bolsheviki and World Peace*, p. 87.
2. Trotsky, *How The Revolution Armed*, vol. 4, p. 119.
3. Lenin, *Collected Works*, vol. 29, p. 549.
4. Two French Communist historians record what their Party's envoy found in Moscow in late May 1940: 'The leaders of the Comintern showed both surprise and disquiet at the military collapse of France'. The USSR 'had obviously wagered on a long war . . . The French *débâcle* upset their prospects.' (F. Crémieux and J. Estager, *Sur le Parti 1939–40* [1983], pp. 216, 227–8).

5. Trotsky (29 July 1924), in *Problems of Civil War* (1970), p. 18.
6. K. Kautsky, *Bolshevism At A Deadlock* (1931), p. 104.
7. G. Ya. Sokolnikov, *Brestskii mir* (1920), p. 28.
8. Lenin, *Collected Works*, vol. 28, p. 19.
9. V. A. Shishkin, *V. I. Lenin i vneshneekonomicheskaya politika sov. gosudarstva, 1917–23* (1977), p. 152.
10. V. G. Bryunin, 'Sov.–germanskie otnosheniya nakanune noyabrskoi revolyutsii', in V. D. Kul'bakin (ed.), *Noyabrskaya revolyutsiya v Germanii* (1960), p. 199.
11. Hoffmann, *War Diaries and Other Papers*, vol. II, p. 347.
12. John M. Thompson, in C. E. Black (ed.), *Rewriting Russian History* (1956), p. 339.
13. Because of public opinion at home, conditioned to loathe anything and anybody connected with 'the old Russia', the Allies were inhibited in their choice of allies among the opponents of Bolshevism. As L. I. Strakhovsky observes (*Intervention at Archangel* [1944], pp. 259–60), 'The greatest tragedy [of the intervention in North Russia] lay in the fact that the Allied governments refused to deal with anyone who was not a *bona fide* democrat or even socialist, while the Russian officers, representing the real active element in the struggle, were overwhelmingly monarchistic.' Commenting on the democratic scruples of the Allies, Ulam notes, regarding the situation at the end of 1918, that, 'in the case of the German high command, the Bolsheviks had confronted an enemy that had been least subject to such scruples and inhibitions: now that enemy was no more' (*Expansion and Co-existence* [1968], p. 93).
14. *Ursachen*, p. 188.
15. P. E. Wright, *At The Supreme War Council* (1921), p. 20.
16. Graham Seton Hutchinson, *Warrior* (1932), p. 271.
17. Correlli Barnett, *The Swordbearers*, p. 341.
18. C. M. E. Mangin, *Comment finit la guerre* (1920), p. 225.
19. Renouvin, *War and Aftermath 1914–1929*, p. 106.
20. Fuller, *Decisive Battles*, p. 276.
21. Robert Blake (ed.), *The Private Papers of Douglas Haig, 1914–1919* (1952), p. 322.
22. J. Terraine, foreword to *Sir Douglas Haig's Despatches* (1979), p. vii.
23. Terraine, *Douglas Haig*, p. 471.
24. Terraine, *To Win A War*, p. 14.

POSTSCRIPT

1. The text of the conversation is in the archives of the West German Foreign Ministry in Bonn. This document is not included in either of the two Soviet publications of relevant diplomatic documents: *Dokumenty vneshnei politiki SSSR* or *Sovetsko-germanskie otnosheniya ot peregovorov v Brest-Litovske do podpisaniya Rapallskogo dogovora*.

Bibliography

Anet, Claude, *La Révolution russe* (4 vols, 1918–19)
Anikeev, V. V., *Deyatelnost Ts.KRSDRP(b) v 1917–1918 gg. Khronika sobytii* (1974)
Anon., 'Further adventures of the armoured cars: Persia and Baku', *Blackwood's Magazine*, March 1919
Antonov, A. V., *Boevoi vosemnadtsatyi god* (1961)
Antonov-Ovseyenko, A. V., *The Time of Stalin: Portrait of a Tyranny* (1981)
Antonov-Ovseyenko, V. A., *Zapiski o grazhdanskoy voine*, vol. II (1928)
Arkhiv Russkoy Revolyutsii, vol. 14 (1924) ('Dokumenty po istorii chernomorskogo flota v marte–yune 1918 g.')
Astrov, E., *et al.*, *Illustrated History of the Russian Revolution* (1928)
Azovtsev, N. N. *et al.*, *Krakh pervogo nashestviya imperialistov na stranu Sovetov* (1973)
Babington, Anthony, *For the Sake of Example: Capital Courts Martial 1914–20* (1983)
Bakhov, A. S., *Na zare sovetskoi diplomatii* (1966)
Baltiiskie moryaki v bor'be za vlast' sovetov (noyabr' 1917–dekabr' 1918) (1968)
Barclay, C. N., *Armistice 1918* (1968)
Barnett, Correlli, *A Military Historian's View of the Great War*, Royal Society of Literature, Essays, New Series, vol. 36 (1970)
——, *The Swordbearers* (1963)
Bauermeister, A., *Spies Break Through* (1934)
Baumgart, Winfried, *Deutsche Ostpolitik 1918* (1966)
——, 'Die "geschäftliche Behandlung" des Berliner Erzählungsvertrag vom 27 August 1918', *Historisches Jahrbuch*, 89 (1969)
——, 'Die Mission des Grafen Mirbach in Moskau, April–Juni 1918', *Vierteljahrshefte für Zeitgeschichte*, 16 (1968)
——, 'Unternehmen "Schlussstein"', *Wehrwissenschaftliche Rundschau*, 19 (1969)
—— (ed.), *Von Brest-Litovsk zur deutschen Novemberrevolution* (1971)
Bazarevskii, A. K., *Mirovaya voina 1914–1918 gg. Kampaniya 1918 goda vo Frantsii i Bel'gii* (2 vols, 1927)
Bečvar, G., *The Lost Legion* (1939)
Beer, Max, *Fifty Years of International Socialism* (1935)
Berlau, A. J., *The German Social-Democratic Party, 1941–21* (1949)
Binding, Rudolf, *A Fatalist at War* (1929)
Biograficheskaya Khronika V.I. Lenina, vol. 5 (1974)
Black, Cyril E. (ed.), *Rewriting Russian History* (1956)
Blake, R. (ed.), *The Private Papers of Douglas Haig, 1914–19* (1952)
Blücher, Princess Evelyn, *An English Wife in Berlin* (1921)
Blumberg, General Sir, H. E., *Britain's Sea Soldiers: A History of the Royal Marines, 1914–1919* (1927)

Bolshevik Propaganda. Hearings before a subcommittee of the Committee on the Judiciary, US Senate, 65th Congress (66th Congress, 1st session, Senate, document no. 62, vol. 3), 1919
Bolsheviks, The, and the October Revolution: Central Committee Minutes for August 1917–February 1918 (1974)
Bonch-Bruevich, V. D., *Vospominaniya o Lenine* (2nd edn, 1969)
Borenius, Tancred, *Mannerheim* (1940)
Borisenko, I., *Sov. respubliki na Severnom Kavkaze v 1918 godu* (1930)
Bothmer, Karl von, *Mit Graf Mirbach in Moskau* (1922)
Bradley, J. F. N., *Allied Intervention in Russia* (1968)
——, *The Civil War in Russia* (1975)
Brandt, Rolf, 'With the Soviet Army', *Living Age*, no. 307 (2 October 1920)
Brook-Shepherd, G., *November 1918* (1981)
Bruun, Geoffrey, *Clemenceau* (1943)
Bubnov, A., S. Kamenev and R. Eideman (eds), *Grazhdanskaya voina 1918–1921 gg.*, 3 vols, 1928–30
Bullock, Alan, *Hitler* (1962)
Bunyan, J. (ed.), *Intervention, Civil War and Communism in Russia, April–December 1918* (1936)
Carley, M. J., 'The origins of the French intervention in the Russian civil war', *Journal of Modern History*, vol. XLVIII (1976), no. 3
——, *Revolution and Intervention: The French Government and the Russian Civil War 1917–1919* (1983)
Carr, E. H., *The Bolshevik Revolution* (3 vols, 1950–3)
——, *German-Soviet Relations between the Two World Wars, 1919–39* (1952)
——, 'Radek's "political Salon" in Berlin, 1919', *Soviet Studies*, April 1952
——, *The Russian Revolution* (1979)
Carrington, Charles, *Soldier from the Wars Returning* (1965)
Carsten, F. L., *The Reichswehr and German Politics* (1966)
Chamberlin, W. H., *The Russian Revolution* (2 vols, 1935)
Cherepanov, A. I., *Pod Pskovom i Narvoi* (1963)
Chicherin, G. V., *Stati i rechi* (1961)
——, *Vneshnaya politika Sov. Rossii za dva goda* (1920)
Chubaryan, A. O., *Brestskii mir* (1964)
——, *V. I. Lenin i formirovanie sovetskoi vneshnei politiki* (1972)
Churchill, Winston, *The World Crisis*, part 2 (1927)
Clements, Barbara Evans, *Bolshevik Feminist: The Life of Alexandra Kollontai* (1979)
Coates, W. P. and Z. K., *Armed Intervention in Russia* (1935)
Crémieux, F. and J. Estager, *Sur le Parti 1939–40* (1983)
Cruttwell, C. R. M. F., *History of the Great War 1914–18* (1934)
Dallin, David, *Russia and Post-War Europe* (1945)
Debo, Richard K., 'The November 1918 teleprinter conversation of Hugo Haase with Georgii Chicherin and Karl Radek: Document and Commentary', *Canadian–American Slavic Studies*, vol. 14, no. 4 (Winter 1980)
——, *Revolution and Survival* (1979)

Debo, Richard K., 'Lockhart Plot or Dzerzhinsky Plot?', *Journal of Modern History*, vol. XLIII, no. 3 (September 1971)
——, 'Litvinov and Kamenev – ambassadors extraordinary', *Slavic Review*, vol. XXXIV, no. 3 (September 1975)
Dekrety sovetskoi vlasti, vol. III (1964)
Delmas, Jean, 'Une mission militaire française à Petrograd après la Révolution d'Octobre', *Revue de Défense Nationale* (June 1966)
Denikin, A. I., *Ocherki russkoi smuty*, vol. III (1924)
Dennis, A. L. P., *The Foreign Policies of Soviet Russia* (1924)
Dernberg, S. *et al.*, (eds), *Sovetsko–germanskie otnosheniya ot peregovorov v Brest-Litovske do podpisaniya Rapallskogo dogovora*, vol. I (1968)
Direktivy Glavnogo Komandovaniya Krasnoi Armii, 1917–1920, vol. I (1969)
Documents on German Foreign Policy (HMSO): 1st series, ii (1948); series D, vol. VIII (1954); and vol. XI (1961)
'Dokumenty po istorii chernomorskogo flota (v marte–yune 1918g.)', *Arkhiv russkoi Revolyutsii 14* (1924)
Dokumenty Vneshnei Politiki SSSR, vol. I (1957)
Erzberger, M., *Souvenirs de Guerre* (1921)
Essame, H., *The Battle for Europe, 1918* (1972)
Ezergailis, A., *The Latvian Impact on the Bolshevik Revolution* (1983)
Fainsod, M., *International Socialism and the World War* (1935)
Falls, Cyril, *The First World War* (1960)
Farrar-Hockley, A., *Goughie* (1975)
Fel'shtinskii, Yu. G., *Bolsheviki i levye esery okt. 1917–iyul' 1918* (1985)
Fic, Victor M., *The Bolsheviks and the Czechoslovak Legion: The Origin of their Armed Conflict, March–May 1918* (1978)
Fischer, Louis, *The Soviets in World Affairs* (2 vols, 1930)
Fischer, Ruth, *Stalin and German Communism* (1949)
Fleming, Peter, *The Fate of Admiral Kolchak* (1963)
Fraiman, A. L., *Revolyutsionnaya zashchita Petrograda v fevrale–marte 1918 g.* (1964)
Freund, Gerald, *Unholy Alliance* (1957)
Fuller, J. F. C., *Decisive Battles, Their Influence Upon History*, vol. II (1940)
Garmiza, V. V., *Krushenie eserovskikh pravitel'stv* (1970)
Gatzke, H. V., *Germany's Drive to the West* (1966 edn)
——, 'Zu den deutsch–russischen Beziehungen im Sommer 1918', *Vierteljahrshefte für Zeitgeschichte*, 3 (1955)
Gilbert, Martin, *Soviet History Atlas* (1979)
Goldsmith, M. and F. Voigt, *Hindenburg* (1930)
Gollin, A. M., *Proconsul in Politics* (1964)
Golovin, N. N., *Rossiiskaya kontr-revolyutsiya v 1917–1918 gg.* (1937)
Goltz, General Rüdiger von der, *Meine Sendung in Finnland und im Baltikum* (1920)
——, *Als politischer General im Osten* (1936)
Golub, P., 'Slavnaya stranitsa internatsionalnoi solidarnosti', *Voenno-istoricheskii zhurnal*, no. 6 of 1965
Gorchenko, A. F. and T. F. Karyaeva, 'Schitayu neobkhodimym vsyacheski usilit Vostochnyi front', *Sov. Arkhivy*, no. 2 of 1980

Gorlov, V. P., *Geroicheskii pokhod* (1963)
Gough, General Sir H., *The March Retreat* (1934)
Grierson, Philip, *Books on Soviet Russia, 1917–1942* (1943)
Griscom, Lloyd, *Diplomatically Speaking* (1941)
Gromyko, A. A. and B. N. Ponomarev (eds), *History of Soviet Foreign Policy*, vol. 1 (1981)
Grondijs, L. H., *La Guerre en Russie et en Sibérie* (1922)
(Haig), *Sir Douglas Haig's Despatches* (1979)
(——), *The Private Papers of Douglas Haig, 1914–1919* (ed. R. Blake, 1952)
Hannington, Walter, *Industrial History in Wartime* (1940)
Hard, W., *Raymond Robins' Own Story* (1920)
Helfferich, K., *Der Weltkrieg*, vol. III (1919)
Herwig, H. H., 'German Policy in the Eastern Baltic Sea in 1918', *Slavic Review*, June 1973
Hilger, G. and A. G. Meyer, *The Incompatible Allies* (1953)
Hill, George, *Dreaded Hour* (1936)
——, *Go Spy The Land* (1932)
Himmer, Robert, 'Soviet Policy towards Germany during the Russo-Polish War, 1920', *Slavic Review*, vol. 35, no. 4 (1976)
Hindenburg, Paul von, *Out of My Life* (1920)
Hinton, James, *The First Shop Stewards' Movement* (1973)
Hoffmann, Max, *War Diaries and Other Papers* (2 vols, 1929)
Hovannisian, R., *Armenia on the Road to Independence* (1967)
Hutchison, Graham Seton, *Warrior* (1932)
Ilyin-Zhenevskii, A. F., *The Bolsheviks in Power: Reminiscences of the Year 1918* (1984)
Ironside, Field-Marshal W. E., *Archangel* (1953)
Israelyan, V. L., 'Neopravdavshiisya prognoz grafa Mirbakha', *Novaya i noveishaya istoriya*, no. 6 of 1967
Jones, David R. (ed.), 'Documents on British Relations with Russia, 1917–1918', *Canadian–American Slavic Studies*, no. 4 of 1974
Jünger, Ernst, *Storm of Steel* (1929)
Kautsky, Karl, *Bolshevism at a Deadlock* (1931)
Kedrov, M. S., *Bez bol'shevistskogo rukovodstva* (1930)
Keep, J. L. H., *The Russian Revolution* (1976)
Kenez, P., *Civil War in South Russia 1918* (1971)
Kennan, G. F., *Soviet–American Relations, 1917–1920*, 2 vols, 1956, 1958 (vol. I: *Russia Leaves The War*; vol. II: *The Decision to Intervene*)
Kessler, Count Harry, *The Diaries of a Cosmopolitan, 1918–1937* (1971)
Kholodkovskii, V. M., *Revolyutsiya 1918 goda v Finlyandii i germanskaya interventsiya* (1967)
Khromov, S. S. (ed.), *Grazhdanskaya voina i voennaya interventsiya v SSSR: Entsiklopediya* (1983)
Koblyakov, I. K., 'Borba sov. gosudarstva za sokhranenie mira s Germaniei v perioda deistviya Brestskogo dogovora', *Istoriya SSSR*, no. 4 of 1958
——, *Ot Bresta do Rapallo* (1954)
Korablev, Yu., *V.I. Lenin i sozdanie Krasnoi Armii* (1970)
——, 'Revolyutsionnaya zashchita Petrograda v fevrale–marte 1918 goda', *Voenno-istoricheskii zhurnal*, no. 11 of 1964

Korablev, Yu., 'V. I. Lenin i organizatsiya otpora voiskam germanskogo imperializma v 1918 goda', *Voenno-istoricheskii zhurnal*, no. 1 of 1968
Kornatovskii, N. A., 'Lenin i Trotsky v borbe s interventami na Murmanske', *Krasnaya Letopis*, no. 3 (36) (1930)
Kovtyukh, E. I., *'Zheleznyi Potok' v voennom izlozhenii* (3rd edn, 1935)
Kozlov, A. I., 'Chernomorskii flot i sov.-germanskie otnosheniya v 1918 godu', *Voenno-istoricheskii zhurnal*, no. 5 of 1984
Krassin, Lubov, *Leonid Krassin* (1929)
Krylenko, N. V., 'Smert staroi armii', *Voenno-istoricheskii zhurnal*, no. 12 of 1964
Kul'bakin, V. D. (ed.), *Noyabrskaya revolyutsiya v Germanii* (1960)
Leggett, George, *The Cheka* (1981)
Lehovich, Dmitri V., *White Against Red: The Life of General Anton Denikin* (1974)
Lenin, V. I., *Collected Works* (4th edn, English version, 1960–70)
Leninskii Sbornik, vol. XI (1931); vol. XXXIV (1942); vol. XXXVII (1970); vol. XXXVIII (1975)
Liberman, S., *Building Lenin's Russia* (1945)
Lieven, Dominic, *Russia and the Origins of the First World War* (1984)
Lifshits, L. M., *Geroicheskii podvig bakinskikh bolshevikov* (1964)
Lipitskii, S. V., *Leninskoye rukovodstvo oboronoi strany* (1979)
——, 'Novyi trud po istorii grazhdanskoi voiny', *Voenno-istoricheskii zhurnal*, no. 1 of 1982
Ludendorff, E. (ed.), *Urkunden der Obersten Heeresleitung über ihr Tätigkeit, 1916–1918* (1921)
——, *My War Memories* (1919)
Lutz, R. H., *The Causes of the German Collapse in 1918* (1934)
——, *The German Revolution* (1922)
Luxemburg, Rosa, *Selected Political Writings* (ed. R. Looker, 1972)
Lyakhov, V., 'Kniga o boevom puti XI Armii', *Voenno-istoricheskii zhurnal*, no. 5 of 1962
MacDonell, Ranald, *'. . . And Nothing Long'* (1938)
Maclaren, Roy, *Canadians in Russia 1918–1919* (1976)
Madelin, Louis, *La Bataille de France* (1920)
Maiskii, I. M., *Vneshnaya politika RSFSR 1917–22* (1922)
Maksakov, V. V. and A. N. Turunov, *Khronika grazhdanskoi voiny v Sibirii, 1917–1918* (1926)
Mandel, David, *The Petrograd Workers and the Soviet Seizure of Power* (1984)
Mangin, General C. M. E., *Comment finit la guerre* (1920)
Mann, Golo, *History of Germany* (1972)
Marchand, René, *Pourquoi je me suis rallié à la formule de la révolution sociale* (1919)
Mashezerskii, V. I., *Pobeda velikogo oktyabrya i obrazovaniye sovetskoy avtonomii Karelii* (1978)
Maslennikov, V. A. (ed.), *Iz istorii agressivnoi vneshnoi politiki germanskogo imperializma* (1959)
Maynard, General G. C. M., *The Murmansk Venture* (1928)
Medvedev, Roy, *Khrushchev* (1982)

Middlebrook, Martin, *The Kaiser's Battle* (1978)
Mints, I. I., *God 1918–i* (1982)
Mirovaya politika v 1924 g. (1924)
Monasterev, N., *Dans la Mer Noire* (1928)
Montgomery, General Sir Archibald, *The Story of the Fourth Army* (1920)
Moore, William, *The Thin Yellow Line* (1974)
Morgan, D. W., *The Socialist Left and the German Revolution* (1975)
Mottistone, Lord, *Adventure* (1930)
Müller, Admiral G. A. von (ed. W. Görlitz), *The Kaiser and his Court* (1961)
Naida, S. F., 'Pochemu Den Sovetskoi Armii i Voenno-Morskogo Flota prazdnuetsya 23 Fevral?', *Voenno-istoricheskii zhurnal*, no. 5 of 1964
Naida, S. F., *et al.* (eds), *Istoriya grazhdanskoy voiny v SSSR*, vol. 3 (1967)
Naudeau, L., *En Prison sous la terreur russe* (1920)
Niessel, General H. A., *Le Triomphe des bolcheviks et la paix de Brest-Litovsk* (1940)
Nikol'nikov, G. L., *Vydayushchayasya pobeda leninskoi strategii i taktiki* (1968)
Norden, Albert, *Zwischen Berlin und Moskau* (1954)
Notovich, F. I., 'Razgrom chetvertogo soyuza v 1918 godu', *Istoricheskii zhurnal*, no. 7–8 of 1941
——, *Razgrom germanskoi armii v 1918 g.* (1941)
Noulens, J., *Mon Ambassade en Russie soviétique* (1933)
Novitskii, General V. F., *Russia and the Allies in the Great War* (1924)
Occleshaw, M. E., 'The "Stab in the Back" - Myth or Reality?', *RUSI*, September 1985
Oliver, F. S., *The Anvil of War* (1936)
Oznobishin, D. V., 'K istoriu bor'by protiv "levykh kommunistov" posle VII s'ezda RKP(b)', *Voprosy Istorii KPSS*, no. 10 of 1969
——, *Ot Bresta do Yur'eva* (1966)
Paquet, Alfons, *Im kommunistischen Russland* (1919)
Petrov, V. I., *Otrazhenie stranoi sovetov nashestviya germanskogo imperializma v 1918 g.* (1980)
Pokrovskii, M. N., *Russia in World History: Selected Essays* (1970)
Possony, S. T., *Lenin, the Compulsive Revolutionary* (1964)
Preobrazhenskii, E. A., *The Third Anniversary of the Russian October Revolution* (1921)
Price, Morgan Philips, *The Origin and Growth of the Russian Soviets* (1919)
——, *The Truth about the Allied Intervention in Russia* (1918 and 1919)
Putyrskii, E. P., *Boevoi Petrograd v 1918 godu* (1972)
Ransome, Arthur, *Autobiography* (1976)
Raskolnikov, F. F., *Tales of Sub-Lieutenant Ilyin* (1982)
Renn, Ludwig, *After War* (1931)
Renouvin, Paul, *War and Aftermath, 1914–1929* (1968)
Repington, C. A'C., *The First World War* (2 vols, 1920)
Ritter, Gerhard, *The Sword and the Sceptre*, vol. II (1973)
Robien, Louis de, *Journal d'un Diplomate en Russie* (1967)
Rosenfeld, Günther, *Sowjetrussland und Deutschland, 1917–22* (1960)
Rostunov, I. I. (ed.), *Istoriya pervoi mirovoi voiny 1914–1918 gg.* (1975)

Rostunov, I. I., *Russkii front pervoi mirovoi voiny* (1976)
Rothstein, Andrew, *The Soldiers' Strikes 1919* (1980)
——, *When Britain Invaded Soviet Russia* (1979)
Rudin, H. R., *Armistice 1918* (1944)
Rutych, N., *Le Parti communiste au pouvoir en URSS, 1917–1960* (1961)
Ryder, A. J., *The German Revolution of 1918* (1967)
Sadoul, Jacques, *Naissance de l'URSS* (1946)
——, *Notes sur la Révolution bolchevique* (1919; reprinted 1971)
Sanders, Michael and Philip M. Taylor, *British Propaganda during the First World War, 1914–1918* (1982)
Schapiro, Leonard, *The Origin of the Communist Autocracy* (2nd edn, 1977)
Scheele, Godfrey, *The Weimar Republic* (1946)
Serge, Victor, *Year One of the Russian Revolution* (1972)
Shcherbakov, A., '"Omolozhenie" legendy', *Voenno-istoricheskii zhurnal*, no. 8 of 1964
Second Congress of the Communist International: Minutes of the Proceedings, vol. I (1977)
Shishkin, V. A., *V.I. Lenin i vneshneekonomicheskaya politika sov. gosudarstva (1917–23 gg.)* (1977)
Smith, C. Jay, *Finland and the Russian Revolution, 1917–22* (1958)
Smogorzewski, K., *La Pologne restaurée* (1927)
Sokolnikov, G. Ya., *Brestskii mir* (1920)
Solomennyi, V., 'Pervyi revolyutsionnyi polk imeni Lenina', *Voenno-istoricheskii zhurnal*, no. 4 of 1962
Solomon, G. A., *Sredi krasnykh vozhdei* (1930)
Solovyov, O. F., *Velikii Oktyabr i ego protivniki* (1968)
Spalding, M. and K. Brooke, *Historical Dictionary of German Figurative Usage*, vol. II (1967)
Stalin, J. V., *On The Great Patriotic War* (1943)
——, *Short Course of History of the CPSU (B)* (English language edn, 1939)
—— *et al.*, *Stalin's Correspondence with Churchill, Attlee, Roosevelt and Truman, 1941–45*, vol. I (1957)
——, *Works* (1952–5)
Steglich, W., *Die Friedenspolitik der Mittelmächte, 1917–1918*, vol. 1 (1964)
Steinberg, I. Z., *Als ich Volkskommissar war* (1929)
Stokesbury, J. L., *A Short History of the First World War* (1981)
Strakhovsky, L. J., *Intervention at Archangel* (1944)
——, *The Origins of American Intervention in North Russia* (1937)
Sukhorukov, V. T., *XI Armiya v boyakh na Severnom Kavkaze i Nizhnei Volge, 1918–20gg.* (1961)
——, 'Tamanskaya Armiya', *Sovetskaya Istoricheskaya Entsiklopekiya*, vol. XIV (1973)
Sulzbach, H., *With The German Guns* (1973)
Sverdlov, Ya. M., *Izbranniye proizvedeniya*, vol. 2 (1959)
Tarle, E. V., *Evropa v epokhu imperializma* (1928)
Terraine, John, *Douglas Haig* (1963)
——, *Impacts of War* (1970)

Terraine, John, *The Smoke and the Fire: Myths and Anti-Myths of War, 1861–1945* (1980)
——, *To Win A War* (1978)
'Times, The', History of, vol. 4 (1952)
Tokoi, O., *Sisu* (1957)
Toland, J., *No Man's Land* (1980)
Tournès, René, *Foch et la Victoire des Alliés, 1918* (*Histoire de la Guerre Mondiale*, vol. 4; 1936)
Toynbee, A. J., *History of the Peace Conference of Paris*, vol. I (1920)
Trotnow, H. *Karl Liebknecht* (1984)
Trotsky, L. D., *The Bolsheviki and World Peace* (1918)
——, *How The Revolution Armed*, vol. I (1979), vol. IV (1981)
——, *On Lenin* (1971)
——, *Problems of Civil War* (1970)
——, *Terrorism and Communism* (1961)
——, *Writings of Leon Trotsky, 1938–39* (1974)
——, *Yevropa v Voine* (1927)
Trukhanovskii, V. G. (ed.), *Istoriya mezhdunarodnykh otnoshenii i vneshnei politiki SSSR 1917–1967 gg.*, vol. 1 (1917–39) (1967)
Ulam, A. B., *Expansion and Coexistence* (1968)
Uldricks, T. J., *Diplomacy and Ideology* (1979)
Ullman, R. H., *Anglo-Soviet Relations, 1917–1921*, vol. I, *Intervention and the War* (1961)
Ursachen des Zusammenbruchs (Reichstag, 12 Ausschuss, 1923, Beilage)
Valluy, J. E., *La Première Guerre Mondiale* (2 vols, 1968)
Vasyukov, V. S., *Predistoriya interventsii* (1968)
Venner, D., *Histoire de l'armée rouge*, vol. I (1981)
Verstraete, M., *Mes Cahiers russes* (1920)
Verzhkovskii, D. V. and V. F. Lyakhov, *Pervaya mirovaya voina* (1964)
Voigt, F., *Unto Caesar* (1938)
Volkonskii, P. M., *The Volunteer Army of Alexeiev and Denikin: a short history from its origin to November 1/14, 1918* (1919)
Volkov, N., 'Deistviya germanskogo flota na morskikh i okeanskikh kommunikatsiyakh Anglii i SShA vo vtoroi mirovoi voine', *Voenno-istoricheskii zhurnal*, no. 5 of 1959
Vospominaniya o V.I. Lenine, vol. III (2nd edn, 1969)
Wheeler-Bennett, J. W., *The Nemesis of Power* (1954)
——, *The Treaty of Brest-Litovsk and Germany's Eastern Policy* (1940)
——, *Brest-Litovsk: The Forgotten Peace* (1938)
Williams, Albert Rhys, *Journey Into Revolution* (1969)
Williams, Jeffrey, *Byng of Vimy* (1983)
Williamson, John G., *Karl Helfferich 1872–1924* (1971)
Wintringham, Tom, *Mutiny* (1936)
Wright, Captain Peter E., *At the Supreme War Council* (1921)
Yakushevskii, A. S., *Propagandistskaya rabota bolshevikov sredi voisk interventov v 1918–20 gg.* (1974)
Zaitsov, A. A., *1918 god* (1934)
Zarnitskii, S. and A. Sergeyev, *Chicherin* (2nd edn, 1975)
Zetkin, Clara, *Reminiscences of Lenin* (1934)

Zharova, L. N. and I. I. Feldman, 'Oborona Khersona vesnoy 1918 goda', *Voprosy istorii*, no. 1 of 1984
Zhilin, P. A. (ed.), *Ocherki po istoriografii sovetskogo obshchestva* (1965)
Zhuravlev, V., *Dekrety sov. vlasti kak istorichesky istochnik* (1979)

Index